# Teaching Creative Writing

by
Melissa J. Donovan

illustrated by
Lori Lawrence

Cover by Janet Skiles

Copyright © Good Apple, Inc., 1990

ISBN No. 0-86653-559-4

Printing No. 987654321

**Good Apple, Inc.**
**1204 Buchanan St., Box 299**
**Carthage, IL 62321-0299**

The purchase of this book entitles the buyer to reproduce student activity pages for classroom use only. Any other use requires written permission from Good Apple, Inc.

All rights reserved. Printed in the United States of America.

# Table of Contents

Unit I Description ........................................................... 1
  Introduction to Description ............................................... 2
  Adjective Charades (warm-up game) ......................................... 3
  In the Way of the Adverb (warm-up game) ................................... 4
    Thesaurus Introduction ................................................. 9
  Thesaurus Work Sheet ..................................................... 10
  Making Thesaurus Crossword Puzzles ....................................... 11
    Thesaurus Crossword Warm-Up ........................................... 12
    Student Directions .................................................... 13
  The Making of a Haunted House (work sheet) ............................... 16
  Multi-Play (game) ........................................................ 17
    Game Words ............................................................ 18
    Student Directions .................................................... 20
    Gameboard ............................................................. 21
  Time for Sentences (work sheet) .......................................... 22
  Creating a Most Vivid Picture for the Reader ............................. 23
  Fun with Advertising in the Town of Typicalville ......................... 32
    Gram's Restaurant ..................................................... 34
    Joe's Outdoor Market .................................................. 35
    Discount Drugstore .................................................... 36
    The General Hardware Store ............................................ 37
    Pet Shop .............................................................. 38
  Introduction to Observation .............................................. 41
    Steps ................................................................. 42
    Poem "A Walk in the Snow" Developed from Observation ................... 44
    How Do People Sleep? (directions) ..................................... 45
    How Do People Sleep? (work sheet) ..................................... 46

Unit II Reader in Mind (RIM) ................................................ 47
  Introduction to Reader in Mind (RIM) ..................................... 48
  How a Fish Can Turn into a Cat ........................................... 49
  Draw-by-the-Description Stories .......................................... 51
    Uthanter .............................................................. 53
    A Wooshy .............................................................. 55
    The Peeper ............................................................ 57
    Potato Head's Invention ............................................... 59

Unit III Characterization ................................................... 61
  Introduction to Characterization ......................................... 62
  Cinderella and Little Red Riding Hood .................................... 63
  Cinderella (story and work sheet) ........................................ 65
  Little Red Riding Hood (story and work sheet) ............................ 67
  Character Research (work sheet) .......................................... 69
  A Ride to the Beach (character dialogue) ................................. 70
  Character traits ......................................................... 72
    Student Resource Sheet (traits) ....................................... 73
    Work Sheet ............................................................ 74
    Work Sheet ............................................................ 75

- Characters (game) .................................................... 76
  - Game Cards ...................................................... 77
  - Student Directions ............................................... 80
- Eight Role Playing Scripts ............................................. 82
- Unit IV Plot Development .............................................. 88
  - Introduction to Plot .............................................. 89
  - Plot Generating .................................................. 90
  - 100 Plot Ideas ................................................... 92
  - Plot Categories .................................................. 95
  - Plot Webs ....................................................... 96
    - Work Sheets ................................................... 97
  - Plot Grid ....................................................... 101
    - Student Directions ............................................ 102
    - Grid ......................................................... 103
    - Plot Cards ................................................... 104
  - Mini Plots ..................................................... 105
  - "My Most Miserable Ten-Year-Old Day" (story developed from mini plot) ............ 110
- Unit V Developing Editing ............................................ 113
  - Introduction to Editing .......................................... 114
  - Steps to Writing Story ........................................... 115
  - Step I, Mini Plot for "Another Old Man and the Sea" ............... 116
  - Step II, Sequence of Events for "Another Old Man and the Seaa" ..... 117
  - Step III, Characterization ....................................... 118
  - Step IV, First Draft for "Another Old Man and the Sea" ............ 120
  - Criteria of Good Writing ......................................... 124
  - Good Writing Criteria with Symbols ............................... 126
  - Editing Reminders/Suggestions .................................... 127
  - Steps V and VI Editing of Story .................................. 128
  - Step VIII Revised Story, "Another Old Man and the Sea" ............ 132
  - Answers ........................................................ 139

# Preface

There are many books on the market today dealing with creative writing. So why do we need another one? This one will actually *teach* students how to write more creatively! Yes, creative writing can be taught. Not simply giving students more things to write on, but instructions and activities that will enhance their creative writing.

The author researched components of good creative writing and what she found was missing in most children's writing. She then designed lessons that would teach these skills. Using them on her own students, she found the results were remarkable improvements in their writing habits. The purpose of this book is to share those methods that worked.

Once students are taught specific criteria of good writing, they then have a reference by which they can compare their own writing and make improvements on it. Five main areas are stressed in this book—a unit is devoted to each one.

DESCRIPTION is explored in the first unit. Students will work on more vivid wording with help from a thesaurus. The young writer will be shown how observation and incubation time can improve one's writing.

RIM (READER IN MIND), a new concept by the author, is explored in Unit II. Students are involved in fun group activities and humorous stories that will help them to understand the necessity of keeping the Reader in Mind when writing. Is the writer creating a picture that is clear enough to make the reader aware of everything going on? While children are working on the activities in this unit, they also will be developing precise vivid descriptions that will emphasize the use of similes and metaphors.

CHARACTERIZATION makes up Unit III. Students are taught how to develop their main characters by giving them appropriate action and dialogue. Class members will have many opportunities to invent action and dialogue for their own portrayal of a specific character.

PLOT DEVELOPMENT in Unit IV helps the student to think of plots while the main emphasis is on the development of plots. The student will learn to visualize everything for the reader, yet not add unnecessary details that will not enhance the plot.

EDITING in Unit V will give the student the opportunity to see how everything learned in the activities in the book will work toward developing a completed story that has been refined. The editing stage will then take place, based on the criteria emphasized in this book. A refined story showing the progressive editing steps that lead to its completion is included.

# Unit I Description

# Introduction to Description

The author feels description is the main key to creative writing. First the writer has to create an accurate picture in the reader's mind, which will serve as a great help in keeping his attention. The challenge for the writer is to picture things clearly, and immediately, because a story must constantly move for the reader. For this to happen, one of the reader's senses must respond at all times. The forming of visual images activates reader's sight and keeps him interacting with the scene and more assures his attention.

The second part of descriptive writing is wording that is enjoyable to read. The overuse and reuse of common everyday words only leads to humdrum writing. Through varying words and adding more vivid words with pizazz, a writer can make his writing come alive and demand the reader to stand up and take notice.

Many approaches and activities found in this unit will help students use more vivid description that will increase the reader's visualization of scenes. Students' writing will become more enjoyable, because overused humdrum words will be replaced with less common words with pizazz.

This unit exposes students to the wonderful world of the thesaurus and the immediate positive effects that can be gained from its use. Some activities will require concentrating their efforts on writing one quality descriptive sentence before advancing into paragraphs and stories. Students will be trained to observe more accurately. Students will have the fun of figuring out a crossword puzzle and designing one of their own. They will have the opportunity to see how the power of good descriptive writing applies to advertising. Descriptive warm-ups reinforcing the use of adjectives and adverbs are included. There is a variety of numerous activities for practice. It is up to the teacher's discretion which ones to use and how many. It is suggested the number of activities correlate with mastery of students' good descriptive writing and applicability in nonguided areas. If more guided practice becomes evident later, the teacher can easily insert almost any activity when and where convenient.

# Adjective Charades

| | |
|---|---|
| Activity: | Students role-play adjectives. They help create mind pictures that will help fellow students to guess the adjectives used. |
| Materials: | pages 5-6, cut up and placed in a container<br>enough space for role playing by children |
| Objectives: | 1. Students will review adjectives as an integral part of descriptive language.<br>2. Used as a warm-up activity to a creative writing assignment, students will let their minds flow more freely and descriptively.<br>3. Students will see the world from a different point of view: that of a flower, tree, lake, etc.<br>4. Students will express themselves descriptively.<br>5. Students will have fun.<br>6. Students will appreciate the effect of adjectives. They help picture things more clearly.<br>7. Students will expand their vocabulary. |
| Directions: | Students take turns drawing slips of paper containing both the adjective and the noun such as "*plump* turkey." The student tells the class the noun "turkey," the word not italicized. Through playacting, other students attempt to guess the adjective. The teacher emphasizes to the students that the adjectives help the actors to create their pictures for the audience by their role playing. The one who guesses correctly may be the next to take a slip of paper and act out the next adjective. |
| Warm-Up: (optional) | The children are asked to stand and act out a branch/stick. The teacher should provide them adjectives that will change the picture. For example:<br>   crooked branch<br>   bent branch<br>   swaying branch<br>   broken branch<br><br>Then the students can become "quiet students sitting down." |
| Comments: | Students will have fun with this one. Many will become motivated enough to think of their own adjectives and nouns to present before the class. Some may accept this additional challenge by making the nouns and adjectives begin with the same letters, such as "*peppy* puppy." Students should be allowed to use their thesauruses for this.<br><br>The most positive outcome of this type of activity is that it can be used as a warm-up for creating more descriptive writing, because the adjectives are very fresh on the minds of these writers. |

# In the Way of the Adverb

**Activity:** Students role-play adverbs. They help create mind pictures that will help fellow students to guess the adverbs used.

**Materials:** page 7, cut up and placed in a container
enough space for role playing by children

**Objectives:**
1. Students will review adverbs as an integral part of descriptive language.
2. Used as a warm-up activity to a creative writing assignment, students will let their minds flow more freely and descriptively.
3. Students will express themselves descriptively.
4. Students will have fun.
5. Students will appreciate the effect of adverbs. They help picture things more clearly.

**Directions:** Students take turns drawing slips of paper containing adverbs and the words they modify such as "*gratefully* giving the baby over to its mother." The student tells the class the words that are not italicized, "giving the baby over to its mother." Through playacting, other students attempt to guess the adverb or how the student is "giving the baby over to its mother." The teacher emphasizes to the students that the adverbs help the actors to create their pictures for the audience by their role playing. The one who guesses correctly may be the next to take a slip of paper and act out the next adverb.

| | |
|---|---|
| *old* man | *upset* baby |
| *stalled* car | *broken* tennis racket |
| *starched* blouse | *obedient* dog |
| *lonely* teddy bear | *shy* girl |
| *enthusiastic* girl | *curious* child |
| *soggy* noodle | *crisp* cookie |
| *melting* snowflake | *sick* child |
| *two-story* house | *crawling* insect |
| *loving* mother | *biting* lobster |
| *hurt* bird | *upside-down* plane |
| *contented* cow | *lumpy* pillow |
| *electric* fan | *friendly* person |
| *handsome* snowman | *skinny* Santa Claus |

| | |
|---|---|
| *raging* river | *pretty* girl |
| *hungry* boy | *runny* nose |
| *steaming* teakettle | *wilting* flower |
| *delicious* shrimp | *heavenly* sunset |
| *refreshing* shower | *conscientious* student |
| *glowing* fire | *reckless* driver |
| *scary* storm | *graceful* dancer |
| *playful* cat | *crashing* wave |
| *teething* baby | *new* car |
| *gigantic* mouse | *thirsty* boy |
| *overcrowded* house | *falling* tree |
| *windy* day | *smooth* lake |
| *deflated* ball | *tangled* shoelace |

| | |
|---|---|
| *proudly* dancing in the recital | *gently* petting the cat |
| *lovingly* caressing the baby | *breathlessly* swimming |
| *busily* making plans for the party | *peacefully* dreaming of a vacation |
| *accurately* shooting baskets | *nervously* taking the test |
| *bravely* attacking the burglars | *cautiously* riding a motorcycle |
| *unhappily* sweeping the floor | *gracefully* skating round the rink |
| *noisily* kissing your spouse | *angrily* walking away |
| *happily* planting flowers | *perfectly* baking a cake |
| *contentedly* reading the newspaper | *carefully* folding the laundry |
| *cautiously* poking the fire | *sloppily* painting the fence |
| *humbly* accepting the award | *triumphantly* rafting down the rapids |
| *absentmindedly* mixing the chemicals | *mischievously* stirring the brew |
| *fairly* playing the game | *enthusiastically* teaching her class |

# Thesaurus Introduction

A most valuable resource and best friend of a writer is a thesaurus with its wealth of synonyms for almost any word in the English language. This book of creative, descriptive and vivid words can make the difference between a creative writer and one less so. It will help writers vary their words to alleviate the humdrum of the same overused words. At the same time, it will greatly expand one's vocabulary.

Students need much practice with the use of a thesaurus to feel comfortable with one and to actualize the effect it has on the reader. The use of the following activities will assure the writer's comfort and the objectives above:

"Thesaurus Work Sheet"
"Making Thesaurus Crossword Puzzles"
"Thesaurus Crossword Warm-Up"
"The Making of a Haunted House"
"Multi-Play" (a thesaurus game)
"Time for Sentences"
"Creating a Most Vivid Picture for the Reader"
"Fun with Advertising"

The author cautions that thesauruses vary in quality. A high quality thesaurus should be considered when purchasing one for classroom use. Otherwise students may become discouraged with their failure to apply it to their needs. Some of the better thesauruses are more difficult to use (cross-referenced), but are well worth the effort.

A good way of introducing students to a thesaurus is to have them peruse a thesaurus and compare it to a dictionary. Students then chart the differences and similarities between them.

The following work sheets and activities purport to expose students to the thesaurus to the level where they will find a comfort with using it every day as most use a dictionary.

Name _____

# Thesaurus Work Sheet

Directions: Look up the overused words below and find more vivid words (related or synonyms) by using a thesaurus. Choose five and write in sentences. Share with class.

| | | | | | | | |
|---|---|---|---|---|---|---|---|
| nice | _____ | pretty | _____ | great | _____ | careful | _____ |
| cold | _____ | cute | _____ | solve | _____ | carry | _____ |
| clean | _____ | good | _____ | mad | _____ | catch | _____ |
| tall | _____ | lot | _____ | all | _____ | clean | _____ |
| soon | _____ | try | _____ | bad | _____ | close | _____ |
| sleep | _____ | cry | _____ | big | _____ | decide | _____ |
| walk | _____ | last | _____ | bug | _____ | deep | _____ |
| break | _____ | happy | _____ | sad | _____ | fall | _____ |
| light | _____ | excited | _____ | every | _____ | fine | _____ |
| fat | _____ | lost | _____ | fight | _____ | now | _____ |
| scare | _____ | gain | _____ | love | _____ | hate | _____ |
| get | _____ | give | _____ | soft | _____ | home | _____ |
| brave | _____ | hit | _____ | hold | _____ | baby | _____ |
| lost | _____ | keep | _____ | kind | _____ | know | _____ |

# Making Thesaurus Crossword Puzzles

| | |
|---|---|
| Activity: | Students will use a thesaurus to design crossword puzzles for their classmates to solve. |
| Materials: | warm-up crossword puzzle on page 12<br>directions on pages 13-14<br>thesaurus<br>large draft paper (Grid duplicated and taped from page 21 works well for making crossword puzzles.)<br>ruler, pencils, etc.<br>copy machine |
| Objectives: | 1. Students will follow sophisticated directions in designing crossword puzzle.<br>2. Students will learn how to make a crossword puzzle.<br>3. Students will apply the use of a thesaurus.<br>4. Students will learn new vocabulary.<br>5. Students will learn more eloquent words to replace everyday common words.<br>6. Students will use thesauruses more by being challenged to solve crossword puzzles. |
| Directions: | Refer to pages 13-14 for specific step-by-step directions. Teacher should guide students through the directions. |

Name _____

# Thesaurus Crossword Warm-Up

Directions: Using the words below, locate synonyms and related words in a thesaurus for your crossword puzzle.

**Across**
1. goals
3. walk
4. let
5. sleep
7. tall
9. cold

**Down**
1. see
2. break
4. group
6. yell
8. mad

# Directions for Making Thesaurus Crossword Puzzle
## (Teacher guidance is suggested.)

1. Gather these materials: pencils, ruler, thesauruses, large paper or grid on page 21.
2. Find a common word in a thesaurus. (old)
   Find a synonym or related word. (patriarchal)
3. Write the new word out on the middle of your paper or grid leaving lots of space for more words that will connect to it.
4. Write the original word you looked up (old) in either a *down* column or an *across* column. (See A.)

A.
```
        patriarchal

Across           Down
old (patriarchal)
```

B.
```
           c
           o
           r
        patriarchal
           u
           p
           t

Across           Down
old (patriarchal)   wrong (corrupt)
```

5. Look up another common word in a thesaurus. (wrong)
   Find a synonym or related word with a letter in common with the first word you put down, which was *patriarchal*. (corrupt)
6. Write the word on your paper so the letter in common will be the connecting link between the two words. (See B.)
7. Write the original word you looked up (wrong) in either the down column or the across column. (See B.)
8. Continue looking up words and finding synonyms or related words with common letters of the words on your paper.

9. When you are all finished with a networking of words, you need to number them appropriately. You number left to right, beginning at the upper left-hand corner. As if you were reading, you move left to right, row to row. Whenever you locate the beginning letter of a new word, that becomes your next number. (See C.)

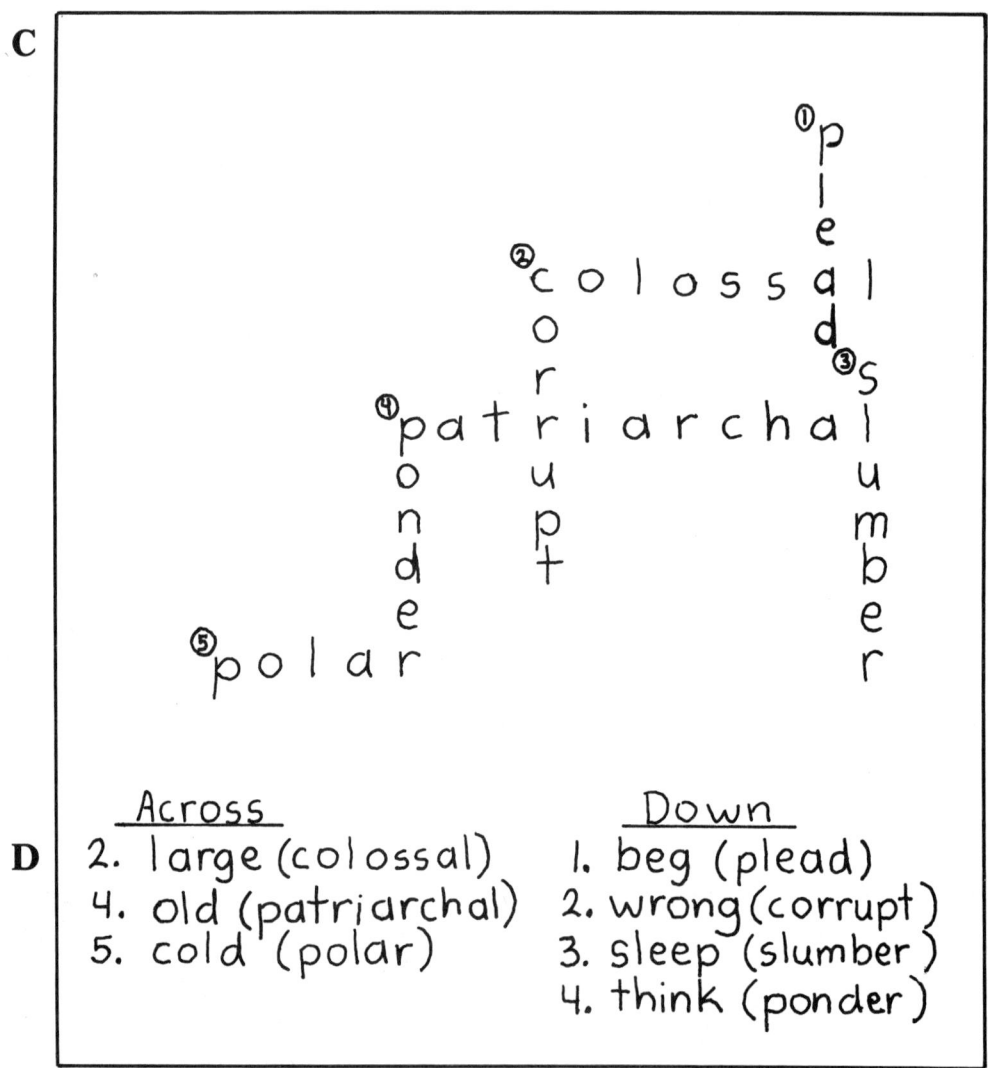

10. Then give your original words numbers that coordinate with the crossword puzzle words. (See D.)
11. Recopy your puzzle neatly with just the grid part around the answer. Be sure to line up your letters carefully. (See E.)
12. If possible, make copies of your crossword puzzle for classmates, friends and parents to solve. If enough students contribute, make a class book.

E

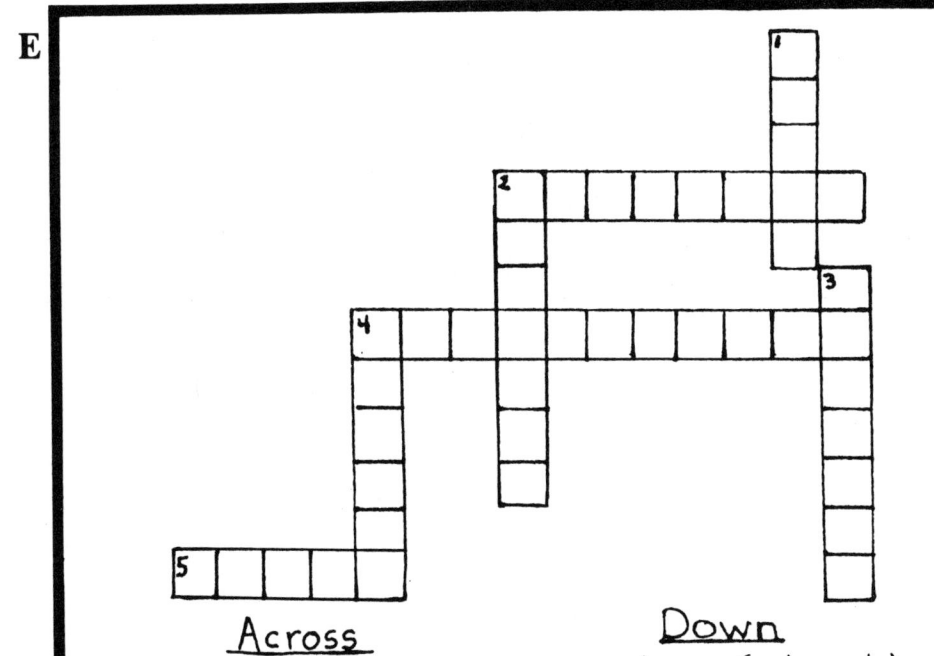

Across
2. large (colossal)
4. old (patriarchal)
5. cold (polar)

Down
1. beg (plead)
2. wrong (corrupt)
3. sleep (slumber)
4. think (ponder)

Name _____

# The Making of a Haunted House

Directions: If you were designing a very scary haunted house, list the contents you would include. Use descriptive words to describe contents. Then using a thesaurus, find more vivid words to give the reader a clearer, more precise picture of your haunted house. Criteria of this assignment: include at least ten items, twenty descriptive words and ten vivid words found in your thesaurus. Create a story or a poem from your list when you are finished.

| Items | More Vivid Description |
|---|---|
| 1. smelly, bubbling witch's brew | pungent, gurgling witch's brew |
| 2. noisy, broken steps | creaking, rotting steps |
| 3. | |
| 4. | |
| 5. | |
| 6. | |
| 7. | |
| 8. | |
| 9. | |
| 10. | |
| 11. | |
| 12. | |
| 13. | |
| 14. | |
| 15. | |

# Multi-Play

| | |
|---|---|
| Activity: | Students will use a thesaurus to find synonyms for a competitive crossword puzzle game. |
| Materials: | thesauruses<br>different color pencil for each player<br>page 21 copied four times and taped for a disposable gameboard<br>letter grid and student directions on page 20<br>words on pages 18-19 copied and cut (May choose to put on heavier board and laminate.)<br>box or large envelope to house game materials |
| Objectives: | 1. Students will review and apply use of the thesaurus.<br>2. Students will learn new vocabulary.<br>3. Students will learn more eloquent words to replace everyday common words. |
| Directions: | Teacher should guide students through the directions. (Refer to page 20 for specific step-by-step directions.) |

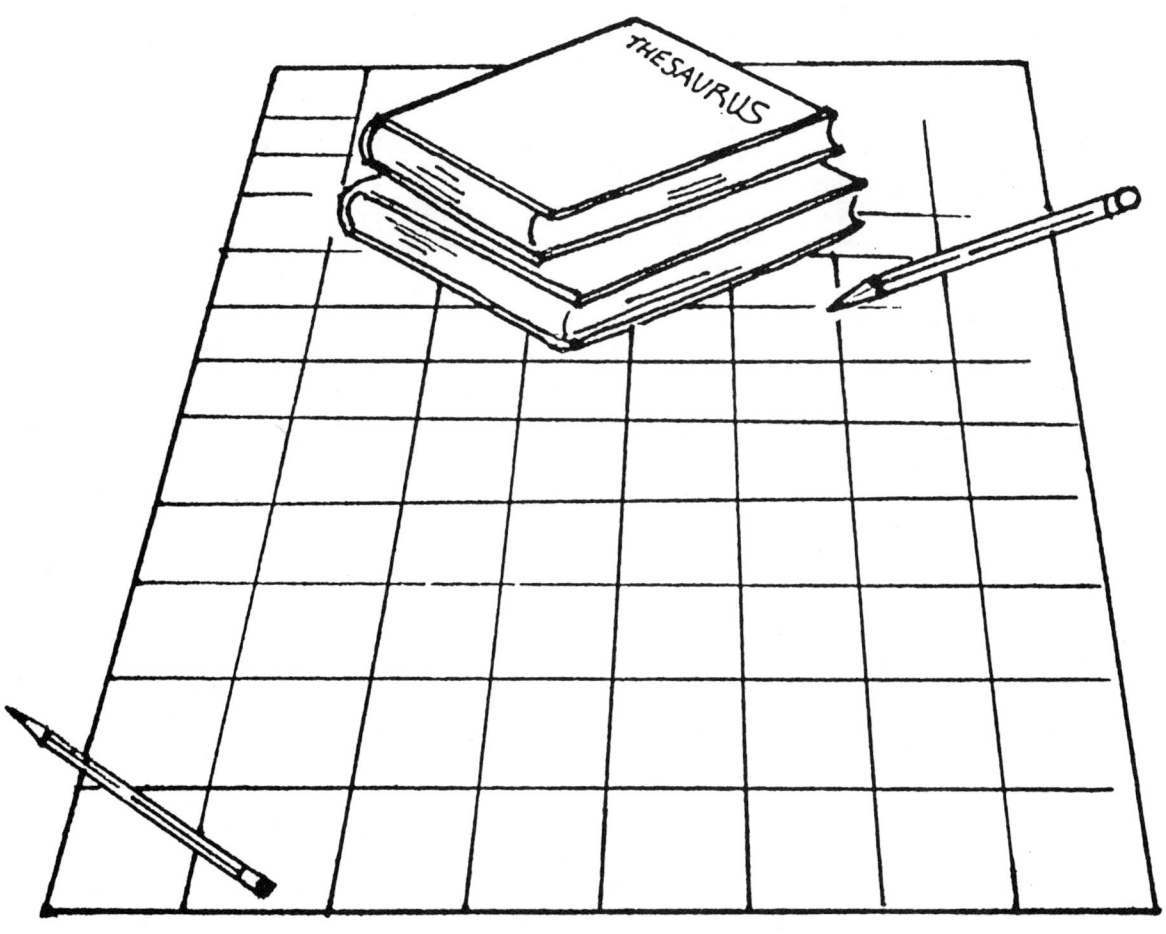

| always | happy | walk |
| --- | --- | --- |
| damp | brave | give |
| dirty | call | yell |
| leave | quiet | look |
| snow | shore | nice |
| sad | manage | wrong |
| sleep | thankful | weed (n) |
| pack | monster | rain (v) |
| pale | use | think |
| plenty | make | pest |

| sell | bit (part) | cold |
| --- | --- | --- |
| windy | careful | upset |
| black | cry | have |
| keep | all right | lost |
| disaster | hurry | excited |
| deep | change (v) | dead |
| cut (v) | break | mad |
| leave (v) | tired | cold |
| get (v) | blue | able |
| fast | different | fix (v) |

# Multi-Play

Materials:
    thesauruses
    different color pencil for each player
    crossword puzzle gameboard
    directions with letter scores
    words on slips of paper or cards, facedown
    paper for keeping score

Objective: To find high-scoring synonym or related word in a thesaurus for your turn writing on the crossword puzzle. The one with the highest score at the end of the game wins.

## Steps of Play

1. All materials are set up for play. Two or more students may play.
2. Someone goes first; it doesn't matter who as long as the same number of turns will be given to each player.
3. Player 1 picks a card and finds a synonym or related word in a thesaurus. First player writes selected word in center of grid. Each letter fits into one square. Score is determined by chart below. (May have three-minute time limit.)
4. Player 2 may either draw another word or use previous player's word. He also finds a synonym or related word. He writes his selected word on the grid. The synonym must be joined with a common letter to form a puzzle.
5. Players continue to find synonyms for a word drawn or from a previous player's word and place it on the grid to form a crossword puzzle. No one player may use the same word he used in the last round.
6. Highest letter score wins game. Game ends at a preset time limit, when someone reaches a certain score (for example, 100) or when players run out of room on grid.

## Suggested Scoring

| | | | | |
|---|---|---|---|---|
| a—1 | g—3 | m—1 | s—1 | y—5 |
| b—3 | h—3 | n—1 | t—1 | z—8 |
| c—3 | i—1 | o—1 | u—1 | |
| d—2 | j—8 | p—3 | v—5 | |
| e—1 | k—5 | q—8 | w—5 | |
| f—2 | l—1 | r—1 | x—8 | |

Directions: For playing board, copy four times and tape together on back.

Name _____

# Time for Sentences

Directions: Rewrite the sentences below using a thesaurus to replace adjectives, adverbs, nouns and verbs. Underline words you've exchanged. You should not, however, change the basic meaning of the sentence.

1. The wicked, old man chased the dirty, shaggy and hungry dog with his crooked cane.

   _____
   _____
   _____

2. The healthy and warmly dressed children withstood unusually low temperatures and blowing snow to build a most handsome snowman.

   _____
   _____
   _____

3. A favorite yearly trip for our family is to the Holland Tulip Festival, where we see lots of beautiful tulips of different colors.

   _____
   _____
   _____

4. The ugly, black spider walked safely around his web, checking his captured, hanging prey.

   _____
   _____
   _____

5. I should have the challenging job. I'm a hard worker, sincere and conscientious, neat and accurate with paperwork, and just a basic, loving, all-around guy.

   _____
   _____
   _____

Copyright © 1990, Good Apple, Inc.　　　　　　　GA1156

# Creating a Most Vivid Picture for the Reader

| | |
|---|---|
| Activity: | Students will describe a picture by writing one clear sentence. Students will rewrite the sentence by replacing words with more vivid words from a thesaurus. |
| Materials: | activity pages 24-31<br>magazine pictures and writing paper |
| Objectives: | 1. Students will try to picture things more clearly for the reader when writing.<br>2. Students will use the thesaurus as a resource.<br>3. Students will learn more vivid wording.<br>4. Students will increase their vocabulary.<br>5. Students will see the value in editing. |
| Directions: | Refer to pages 24-31 for specific directions. Students look at a picture from one of the following pages. They write a description of the picture in one sentence. "A very cute, white rabbit was sitting in the soft snow." Adjectives should be included if it enhances the description. Students should be encouraged to write so someone could picture it in his mind by just hearing the sentence. |
| Extension: | Students may use magazine pictures of their own choosing and do the same type of activity. The pictures and sentences could then be displayed to be shared by all. A bulletin board with the title Most Vivid Descriptions or The Effects of a Thesaurus will enhance the display. |

Name _____

# A Most Vivid Picture

Directions: Write a descriptive sentence of the picture so the reader will be able to picture it in his mind. Then rewrite it by replacing words with more vivid words from a thesaurus. Underline replaced words.

Original: _____

_____

_____

Rewritten: _____

_____

_____

Name _____

# A Most Vivid Picture

Directions: Write a descriptive sentence of the picture so the reader will be able to picture it in his mind. Then rewrite it by replacing words with more vivid words from a thesaurus. Underline replaced words.

Original: _____
_____
_____

Rewritten: _____
_____
_____

Copyright © 1990, Good Apple, Inc.  GA1156

# A Most Vivid Picture

Directions: Write a descriptive sentence of the picture so the reader will be able to picture it in his mind. Then rewrite it by replacing words with more vivid words from a thesaurus. Underline replaced words.

Original: _____

_____

_____

Rewritten: _____

_____

_____

# A Most Vivid Picture

**Directions:** Write a descriptive sentence of the picture so the reader will be able to picture it in his mind. Then rewrite it by replacing words with more vivid words from a thesaurus. Underline replaced words.

Original: _____

Rewritten: _____

Name _____

# A Most Vivid Picture

Directions: Write a descriptive sentence of the picture so the reader will be able to picture it in his mind. Then rewrite it by replacing words with more vivid words from a thesaurus. Underline replaced words.

Original: _____
_____
_____

Rewritten: _____
_____
_____

Name _____

# A Most Vivid Picture

Directions: Write a descriptive sentence of the picture so the reader will be able to picture it in his mind. Then rewrite it by replacing words with more vivid words from a thesaurus. Underline replaced words.

Original: _____

_____

_____

Rewritten: _____

_____

_____

Name _____

# A Most Vivid Picture

**Directions:** Write a descriptive sentence of the picture so the reader will be able to picture it in his mind. Then rewrite it by replacing words with more vivid words from a thesaurus. Underline replaced words.

Original: _____

_____

_____

Rewritten: _____

_____

_____

Name _____

# A Most Vivid Picture

Directions: Write a descriptive sentence of the picture so the reader will be able to picture it in his mind. Then rewrite it by replacing words with more vivid words from a thesaurus. Underline replaced words.

Original: _____

_____

_____

Rewritten: _____

_____

_____

# Fun with Advertising in the Town of Typicalville

# Fun with Advertising

Activity: Using a thesaurus to find more vivid and exciting words, students will rewrite advertisements for different products in the stores of Typicalville. They also will create ads of their own from scratch.

Materials: pages 34-38 (Each page includes items for sale from individual merchants.) thesauruses

Objectives:
1. Students will use a thesaurus as a resource.
2. Students will learn more vivid and exciting wording.
3. Students will increase their vocabulary.
4. Students will be exposed to advertisements and the value of description.

Directions: Refer to pages 34-38 for specific student directions. There are five pages dealing with advertising from different merchants in a small town. Students will have the opportunity to rewrite ads and design new ones for Gram's Restaurant, Joe's Outdoor Market, a hardware store, a pet shop and a drugstore. It is suggested students bring in advertisements on their favorite products for discussion in preparation for this assignment. Teacher should reinforce how a thesaurus can help.

Name _____

# Gram's Restaurant

Directions: Make improvements in Gram's ad by replacing words with more vivid words from a thesaurus.

**Menu**

Visit Gram's Restaurant and you'll be graciously served in a warm, friendly atmosphere. Select from Gram's fine menu of crisp, fresh salads, delicious hot main courses, and fluffy moist desserts.

Use a thesaurus to help you describe some of Gram's special menu items.

| | | | | | |
|---|---|---|---|---|---|
| _____ | _____ | soup | _____ | _____ | omelet |
| _____ | _____ | pie | _____ | _____ | pancakes |
| _____ | _____ | turkey | _____ | _____ | cake |
| _____ | _____ | dressing | _____ | _____ | ham |
| _____ | _____ | potato salad | _____ | _____ | pot roast |
| _____ | _____ | pudding | _____ | _____ | hamburgers |
| _____ | _____ | muffins | _____ | _____ | fried chicken |

Name _____

# Joe's Outdoor Market

Directions: Make improvements in Joe's ad by replacing words with more vivid words from a thesaurus.

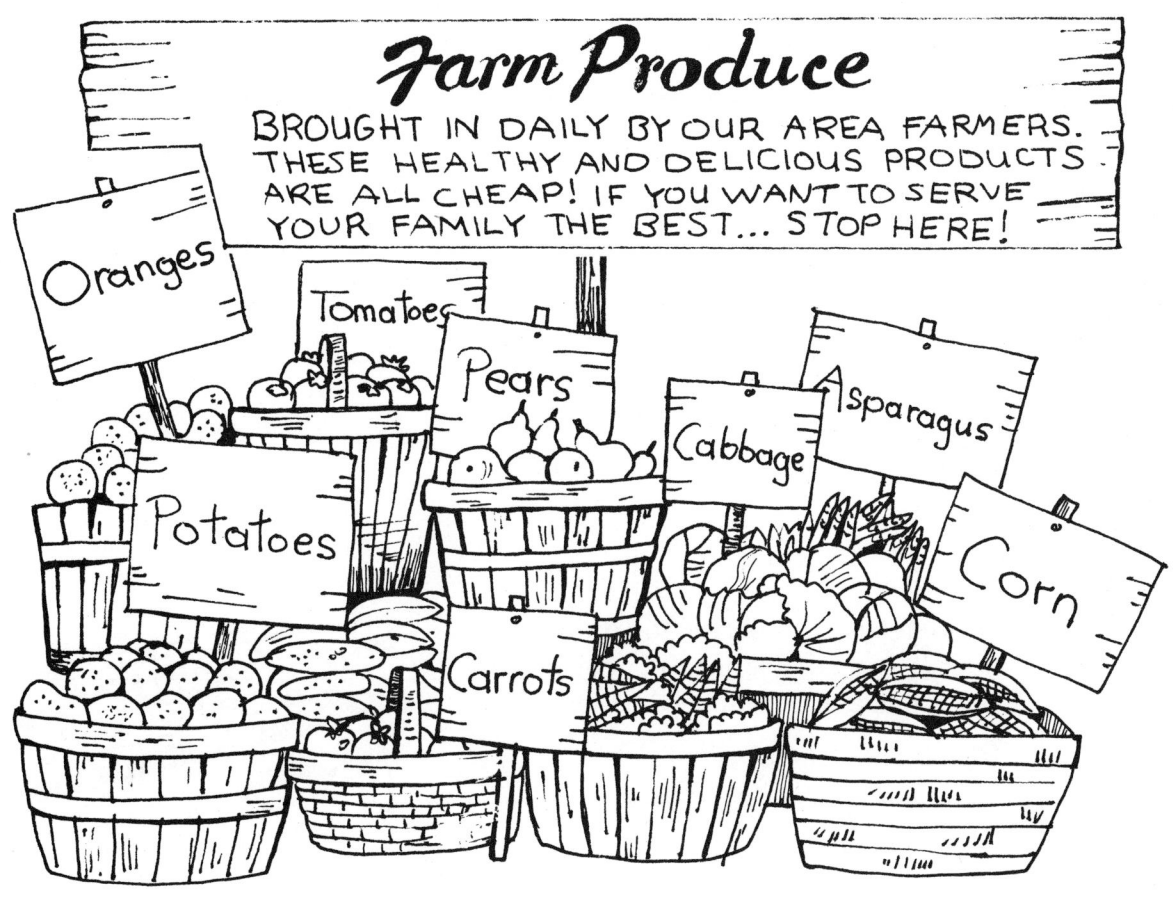

Use a thesaurus to help you describe some of Joe's weekly specials.

| | | | | | |
|---|---|---|---|---|---|
| _____ | _____ | tomatoes | _____ | _____ | squash |
| _____ | _____ | corn on cob | _____ | _____ | potatoes |
| _____ | _____ | asparagus | _____ | _____ | cantaloupe |
| _____ | _____ | strawberries | _____ | _____ | blueberries |
| _____ | _____ | peaches | _____ | _____ | cider |
| _____ | _____ | oranges | _____ | _____ | cheese |
| _____ | _____ | eggs | _____ | _____ | bouquet of flowers |

Name _____

# Discount Drugstore

Directions: Make improvements in the ads below by replacing words with more vivid words from a thesaurus.

Snuffle Plus syrup is a cool, soothing liquid that calms that nagging, annoying cough.

_____
_____
_____
_____
_____

For gleaming white teeth and fresh breath, so you'll capture a delicious kiss from that handsome man of your dreams, try Charisma Power Toothpaste, either bright red gel or blue-dotted white paste.

_____
_____
_____
_____
_____

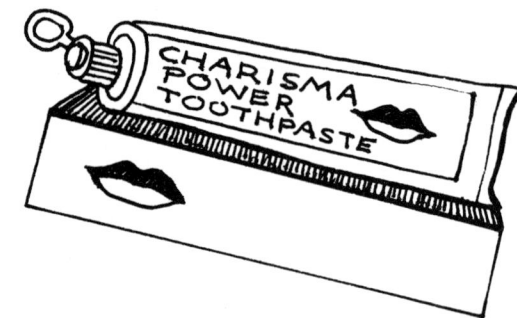

For a quick pick-me-up, bite into a delicious, crunchy, yet nutritious, Mellow Nut candy bar that's filled with creamy peanut butter, smooth chocolate, fluffy and light marshmallows and crisp pecans.

_____
_____
_____
_____
_____

# The General Hardware Store
## Special Sale

Directions: Make improvements in the ads below by replacing with more vivid words from a thesaurus.

Wonder vacuum cleaner. It sweeps up crumbs and other small things, mops up liquid spills, licks up caked on mud, picks up left out toys, fluffs up matted down carpet, and coughs up sweet fresh air!

Dinoraft: Strong raft shaped like your favorite loveable dinosaur. Your child will have hours of fun rocking back and forth on this incredible water toy.

Directions: Make original advertisements for the following items. Then replace words with more vivid words from a thesaurus. Option: Find pictures of similar ads and display with your ads on a bulletin board.

out-of-season snowblower
bag of weed killer
bug repellent
tennis racket
paint supplies
pup tent

lawn chair
birdhouse
clock radio
lawn mower
portable grill

Name _____

# My Pal Pet Shop

Directions: Make improvements in the ads below by replacing words with more vivid words from a thesaurus.

Soft, furry kittens for sale. These cute, loving kittens will give you nothing but love and enjoyment.

_____
_____
_____
_____

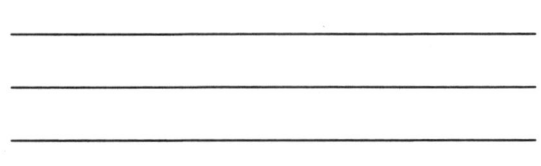

There also are plenty of fun, playful puppies. They are just waiting for a warm, caring home.

_____
_____
_____

If poor old Rover is bothered by little black, biting fleas, then sprinkle him with Flea Freedom Flea Powder, and all his fleas will be killed instantly.

_____
_____
_____
_____

Try writing your own ads from scratch on the following: parrot, exotic fish, guppies, dog basket, hamsters, aquariums, dog sweaters, cat toys, Pet Gourmet Delight Food.

# More Ideas for Using the Thesaurus in the Classroom

1. (To be used with the computer/word processor and/or computer programs where students design pictures and write stories.) On computers, students write descriptive sentences of their pictures as in the activity on page 23. Then they rewrite their sentences using more vivid words from a thesaurus; some word processors have built-in thesauruses.

2. Teacher or students select an overused word for the week (for example, *cold* in December). Students find related or similar words in a thesaurus and use them in their speech. Every time they use a word (*polar*) or recognize someone else using a more vivid word, they may have a point for individual charting.

3. Students bring in examples of favorite descriptive words they find in magazines and newspapers and share with other members of the class. Class may discuss meanings of words and how the descriptive words improved the writing. Articles and underlined words can be displayed as a bulletin board/learning center with caption Words Add Pizzazz.

4. Students work on describing something (a picture of a Big Mac, wintry scene) by making a list of descriptive words. They then use a thesaurus to enhance their lists. After each student has completed his list, he shares his favorite description with the members of the class.

5. (Elaboration of #4) Given a theme, story, etc., students list important symbols/nouns. Symbols of winter may elicit *snowflake, snowman, fireplace, cocoa, icicle*. In teams, students make large pictures of their nouns. They then brainstorm adjectives, with the use of the thesaurus, that describe their symbols. They select from their long list fifteen or so that they think are the best. On pieces of paper they write their words (for example, *scrumptious cocoa*) and add them to their pictures. The teacher should encourage students to use all senses (for example, *snapping fire, slippery icicle*). This is an excellent activity for use with language arts, drawing a main character and adding adjectives describing his personality.

6. As part of writing assignments, the teacher expects so many words (3-5) replaced by using a thesaurus, indicating the more vivid ones looked up by underlining.

# Introduction to Observation

The author feels there are many similarities between good artwork and good writing. The writer, like the artist, captures the details of life and paints a scene for the reader or viewer. To do this, you have to observe carefully what is out in our world as Norman Rockwell did. His characters have wrinkled and weathered hands, frowned brows and wispy hair. They are clothed in patched and suspendered jeans, holey sweaters, showing slips and too-short-of-sleeves. His rooms have chipped wallpaper, newspapers strewn around and toys left out. Old neighborhoods have wash hanging, dogs barking, mailmen delivering and children romping.

We can't add descriptive detail to our writing unless we ourselves know what's in a scene. Part of this just involves "taking the time to smell the flowers." This involves taking the time to observe. Observation* is the act of looking closely at something. The inclusion alone of this important component, observation, will help because students will be given the time to look to see what's really in a scene. And then look again to see what they missed the first time. In the next several pages, the author will take this reader through simple observation steps to illustrate how it can enhance writing.

The last part of observation suggests that teachers illustrate observation with students' own artwork. It is of interest to analyze students' drawings of a scene of children tumbling down a hill. How many students keep all shirts and pants in tact as if there wasn't such a thing as gravity? Does anyone actually put himself at the scene* and observe what he really might see—a bare stomach, for example? Assigning students to observe and/or visualize first will enhance artwork as well as writing.

*Visualization is used by the author in conjunction with observation. It is the act of seeing something in your mind. Visualization may be used by students if they have already been exposed to a scene. It involves going through your mind and taking time to remember details of the scene called for.

# Observation Steps

Step I: The teacher presents the assignment (though it will not be written for a day or two) and directions on what should be observed to prepare students for their assignment. If possible, bring in comparisons:
"What Makes a Winter Day in Michigan?" (vs. in Florida)
"What Makes a House Haunted?" (vs. your house)
"What Makes a Hyped-up City?" (vs. the peaceful countryside)

Step II: Students go to scene (may bring in movie) and write down things/details that make their scene.

Step III: The teacher conducts a class brainstorming session that yields a list of observations on the chalkboard. Someone copies it down and the teacher makes a copy for each student.

Step IV: Students go to the scene and look again. They look for things they did not notice before. (Teacher may opt to include sounds.)

Step V: Add description. Use thesaurus.

Step VI: Incorporate the best from your list into a theme paper or poem.

# Observation Step Examples

Step I: Assignment: poem on "Winter in Michigan"

Steps II: Class' brainstormed list (first time)
and III:
- warmly dressed children
- white snow
- snow piles
- falling snow
- snowmen
- boots, hats, mittens
- skiing, skating, snowmobiling
- people shoveling walks
- snowplows
- trees covered with snow
- icicles
- frozen lakes
- snowflakes
- earmuffs
- sledding
- ice fishing
- cars stuck

Steps IV: Added list after being sent out one more time and some help from a thesaurus
and V:
- dripping icicles
- cool crisp air
- footprints in the snow
- skeletal trees
- bundled tots
- rosy cheeks
- vaporized breaths
- chimney smoke
- crunchy snow
- everything's white
- days shorter/nights longer
- glistening rays on a glassy covered pond
- barren nests
- no birds
- no insects, butterflies or flowers
- white fluffy snow all around, coming down
- long johns

# A Walk in the Snow

Long johns on—it's out into the cold,
Zip up, bundle up, yippee, there's snow.
One step forward; gee I can't move.
Up, down, up, down, soft to crunchy snow

    Up, down, up, down,
    Plowing through,
    Huff puff, huff puff,
    A rest due.

Phew, take a breath and look at the sights;
Ah-h-h backgrounds of white; things stand out bright—
Frosted skeletal trees and white fluffy down,
Delicate flakes coming down, coming down.

    They dance, they prance
    to the ground;
    They dance, they prance
    all around.

The sun's rays glisten; no they shimmer
On the frozen glassy covered pond;
Hanging icicles flow from above
Chiming a tune rooftop to rooftop.

    Sparkle, sparkle
    drip, drip, drip
    Sparkle, sparkle
    drip, drip, drip

Sightseeing over, it's time for play;
People are snowmobiling; they're sledding.
They are skiing, skating, and sleighing;
It's fun-filled time in cool crisp air.

    Coasting, gliding
    Swish, swish, swish
    Coasting, gliding
    Swish, swish, swish

Hey there's Frosty, Frosty the snowman,
And there are bundled tots with rosy cheeks;
Their mittens softly pad him plump,
Fatter, fatter so he will keep.

    Charcoal, corncob pipe,
    button nose,
    Long scarf, mittens,
    Ooh my toes.

Brrr it's getting late; it's time to go;
Chimneys keep smoking, hearths keep glowing;
Flickers of light warm this precious sight,
Never forgetting, I'll say good night.

# How Do People Sleep?

Activity: After being exposed to the topic of sleeping, students will draw someone sleeping. They will add detail based on observation and/or visualization.

Materials: page 46
may prefer to draw on construction paper
place to display pictures for enjoyment and discussion

Objectives:
1. Students will realize the positive effects of observation and visualization.
2. Students will spend more time observing and/or thinking about a scene before drawing or writing.

Directions: Teacher assigns page 46, "How Do People Sleep?" Students can warm up to the activity by discussing how they sleep. Role playing their sleep may bring much humor to the activity. Another option is to have students research, prior to their drawing, people actually sleeping. After much thought on subject and observation, students should each draw someone sleeping. The teacher should put pictures up so students can look for detail that reflected good observation— true to life yet original.

    cat sleeping in someone's arms
    man sleeping with his mouth open or toes sticking out of the covers
    book left open; light left on

Teacher should reinforce that observation and visualization ahead of the drawing lead to detail and originality of the pictures.

Extension: Other interesting scenes that require detailed observation may be drawn. Some suggestions include a scene of
1. beach or pool
2. woods
3. school lunchroom
4. office
5. elevator in a big department store
6. bleachers during a baseball game
7. baby's first Christmas
8. a zoo
9. career
10. anthill

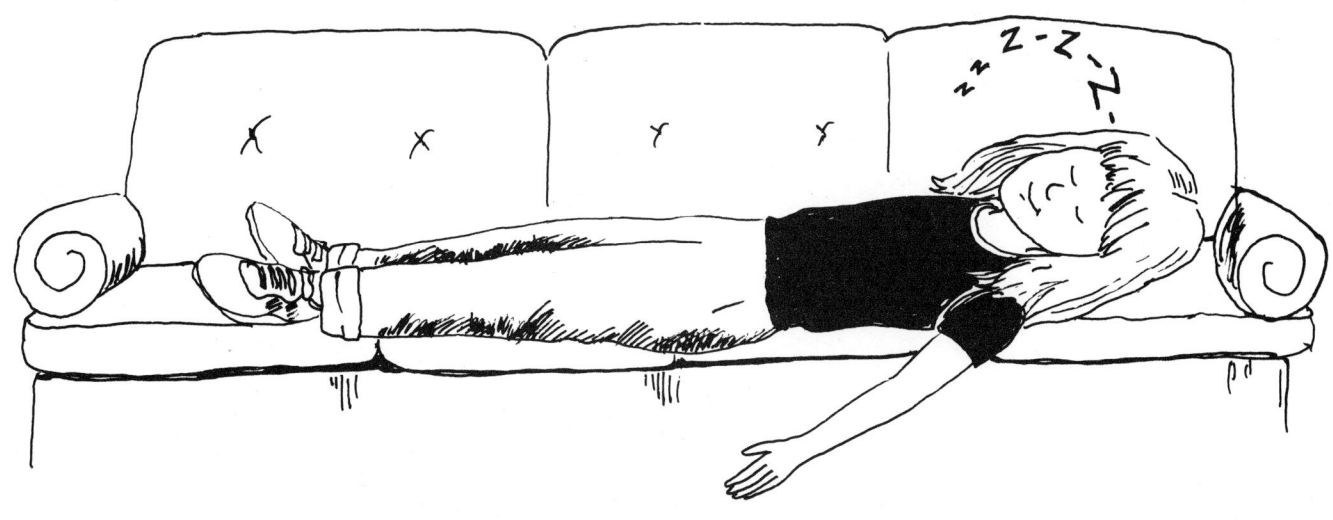

Name _____

# How Do People Sleep?

Directions: Think of all the ways you sleep. Think about other people you have seen sleeping. Maybe you want to research by observing sisters and brothers. Look for detail that would add interest to someone sleeping. Draw someone sleeping below. Include detail of interest. Try to come up with original but realistic detail that no one else thinks of.

After all classmates' pictures are hung up, enjoy and discuss them. Which ones have detail you observed or visualized? Which ones have detail you had not thought of? Which ones have detail that is original?

Optional: Write a story about sleeping.

# Unit II Reader in Mind

# Introduction to Reader in Mind (RIM)

Good communication takes place when the writer and reader see the same picture. The writer first needs to be aware that the reader sees a blank slate until the writer does picturing through his descriptive language. It is important that the young writer is made aware of this so he becomes much more precise with his descriptive language. He needs to keep the reader in mind (RIM).

This unit is composed of humorous stories which the teacher reads to her students. Near the completion of each story, a creature appears. Under normal circumstances, the author would describe it so the readers could picture it in their own minds. The author already visualizes the particular character, scene or whatever, because he or she created the creature. Since the reader only sees it through the eyes of the author, description is very important.

For these stories the description of the characters/creatures has been purposely omitted. Rather, the entire class (with the exception of the child who is the reader) will become the writer and is shown a large picture of the creature. The reader at the chalkboard will draw it as described by his class. As this type of activity is repeated and class description improves, it will become easier for the reader to draw the picture. The writers will gradually see the importance of using descriptive language. Becoming more conscious of it is the first step to more descriptive writing.

# How a Fish Can Turn into a Cat
## (Student RIM Introduction)

This initial activity will help show students how important it is to keep the reader in mind (RIM) when writing, or the reader will see something different than the author had in mind.

Directions: The teacher shares the following story and draws sequential pictures on the board. The teacher needs to preface story with "Describing is very important when you are communicating to others. If you are not careful with your description, things can become confusing." At the end of the story, teacher and class discuss RIM (Reader in Mind) and how the reader (Little Brother) didn't see the same thing as writer (Big Brother). The class may give suggestions as to how Big Brother could have made it clearer for Little Brother, but at this point the author doesn't feel it necessary.

## Story

There once was a little boy who didn't know what a fish looked like, so he asked his brother to describe one for him, and this is what went on. (Now remember the little boy sees nothing, like a blank slate, until someone describes something.)

D. Big Brother says, "It has fins." And realizing his brother was having difficulty seeing what he was describing, he tried to be more careful with his description, so he added, "You know, two pointed things." But lo and behold it was too late.

Teacher draws.

B. It, of course, has a head. Little Brother sees.

Teacher draws.

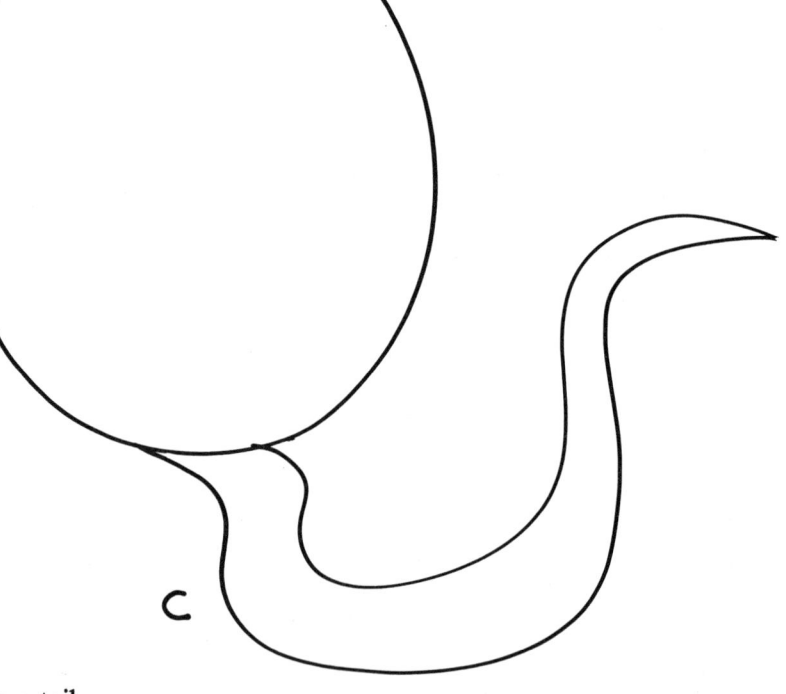

A. Big Brother said, "Well it has a round body." Little Brother sees.

Teacher draws.

C. Oh, and it has a tail. Little Brother sees.

Teacher draws.

And Little Brother saw a cat and thought he saw a fish!

# Draw-by-the-Description Stories

Activity: Student draws a character by the class' description.

Materials: pages 53, 55, 57 and 59 drawn on large poster board
chalkboard, chalk
easel for holding poster (Easel needs to be placed in front of chalkboard so student at board, who is drawing, cannot see it.)
pages 54, 56, 58 and 60 (stories to be read by teacher prior to showing the poster)

Objectives:
1. Students will think about how the reader will perceive their ideas when writing.
2. Students will be more descriptive.
3. Students will realize there is more to writing than being creative. You have to put your creative ideas down so others will see the same thing you intended them to see.
4. Students will review similes and metaphors.

Directions: The teacher reads one of the stories to the class. Prior to reading, one student is selected to come to the chalkboard. At the end of the story is a creature that is unusual. Description is not included with the story, but there is a picture which the teacher will enlarge. At the end of the story, she shows it to the class. The student at chalkboard is not allowed to see the picture. Class members become the writers and describe the creature for the person at the chalkboard.

That person is like the reader. He can only picture what the writers describe. It should be stressed that it is important for the writers to be as clear as possible so reader sees the picture they do.

Class description should sound something like this: "His head is like a pumpkin."

"His head is like an upside down cracked light bulb."

Copyright © 1990, Good Apple, Inc.

It is important to remember that the reader does not see the actual picture and has to follow these rules:

1. Reader (at chalkboard) cannot erase once image is drawn on board.
2. He may not ask any questions, such as "Do you mean this?" because the reader doesn't normally get the opportunity to ask the author such questions.
3. No hand motions are to be used in describing, because that isn't part of writing.

At the end of the drawing, the student artist gets to see the real creature. In the beginning there may be much discrepancy until students become more precise with their descriptions. It should be stressed by the teacher that this is not the fault of the drawer. He just "pictured" what the class described. This is the time to elaborate again on the importance of being more exact for the reader. Description improves with the increase of this type of activity.

# Uthanter

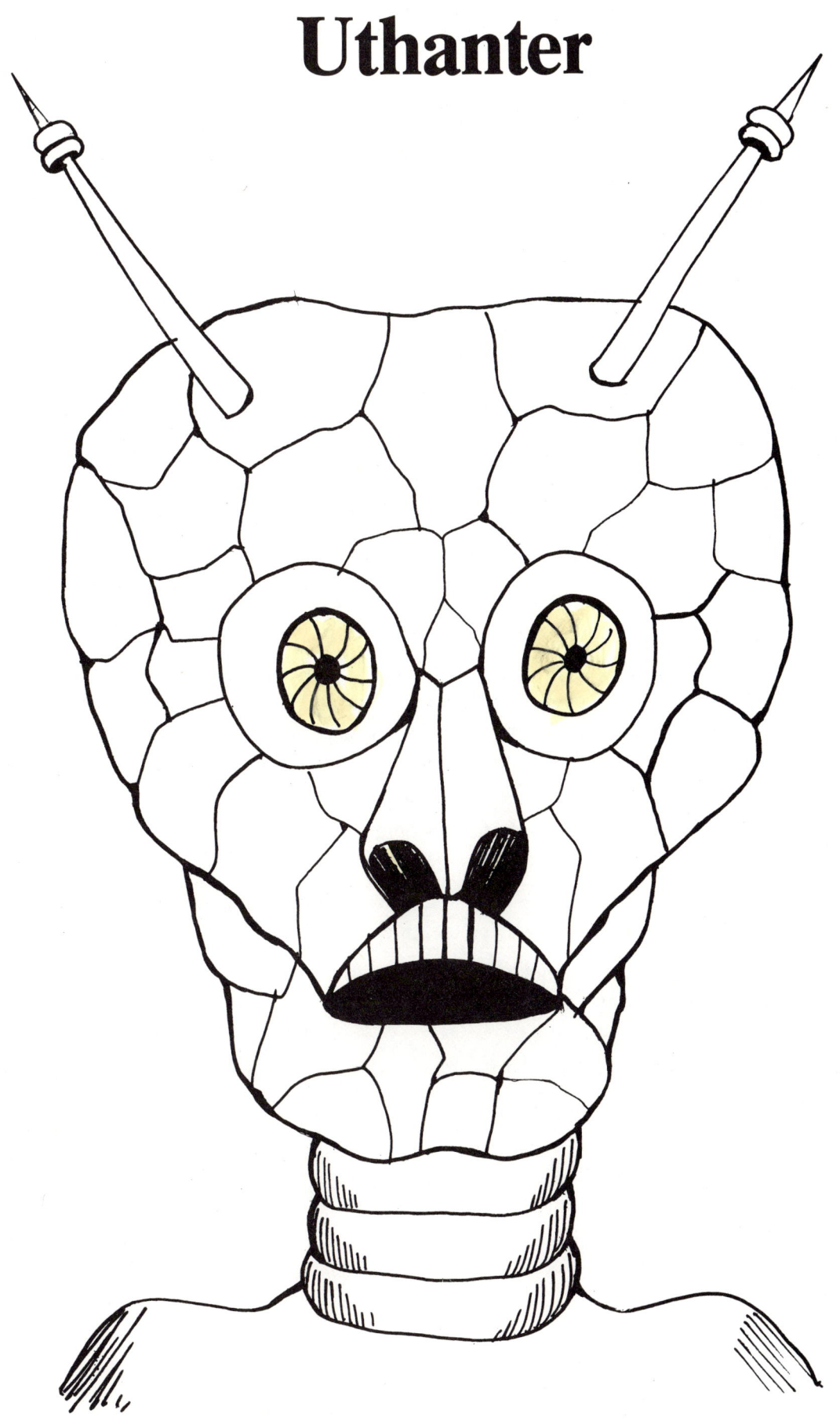

# Uthanter

Uthanter was exhausted and scared. The spaceship he was on decided to make a stop on the planet Earth. He didn't understand, but it took off without him—leaving him alone on Earth. The space crew must not have realized he got off the ship to see what Earth was like. Well, now he was going to find out.

He'd been in the wooded area for the night and all day. Now he was ready to see if he could find some creatures like himself. From the edge of the woods, he saw creatures going in and out of large structures—probably their living quarters. He decided to go closer to one of the structures to have a better look.

He tapped on a window. He was so excited to see someone. He pressed his head as close to the windowpane as possible so he could see the living beings within.

"Must be the wind," said Mrs. Jackson. "I'll just check the window."

"Oh, goody-goody! It's coming! It's coming!" thought Uthanter to himself.

"Mrs. Jackson cupped her eyes with her hands and pressed them to the window. So did Uthanter. Her eyes became very big. Her mouth opened so wide, most of her face disappeared, and she didn't move. She seemed stuck to the window. Uthanter didn't know what to do.

Then he heard from within, "Mom, Mom, are you all right? Why aren't you moving?" said one of the three little upright creatures coming towards Mom. The three looked out, yelled "E-e-e-e-e-e-k!" and dragged their mom out of sight into another room.

Uthanter started pounding on the window—his way of saying "Please help me; please help me! I just want to go home!" He sat down in the wet grass to think about his problem. Why wouldn't they let him in? Why did they run? He just wanted a companion—or someone that would help him find his home. He began to whimper, "I want to go home. I want to go home."

All of a sudden he heard the terrible sound of sirens, and lights began flashing all around blinding him. He was so scared he took off again for the woods to find a place to hide.

After things had quieted down, Uthanter went back to the house. Even though he was scared, his drive for communication with another living creature was even stronger.

This time he just raised his head enough to the window to see what was happening. Mom was seated across two bigger creatures who were taking notes. "He, it, whatever it was, was just terrible looking," said Mom.

"Would you please describe him for us, Mrs. Jackson?" said one of the uniformed creatures.

Uthanter sat slowly down under the window so he could hear this frightening description of himself. He began realizing why they were afraid of him as they described him.

"Well, he looked . . . ." (Describe Uthanter so the reader will be able to picture him in his/her mind.)

# A Wooshy

# A Wooshy

Mrs. Hypo, Billy's teacher, said to her class, "Today we're going to try a different kind of show and tell. I want everyone to share the most unusual thing he's ever seen. "Who would like to begin?"

"Oh, brother," thought Billy. "Hands are already waving."

Billy began to think of what he possibly could share. He remembered the time he was sure he saw a UFO with kaleidoscopic lights that made the whole sky look like a rainbow—this one particular night. But then—hasn't everyone, at one time or another, thought he saw a UFO? No big deal. He'd just have to think of something else.

There was the time he found a cave and saw the most beautiful glass icicle hanging from the ceiling. He knew it was either called a stalactite or a stalagmite, but he couldn't remember which, and they had studied that in class, too. He didn't want to be laughed at if someone remembered which was which—like maybe his teacher who seemed to know everything he didn't. No—he'd just have to think of something else. But what?

There was the time a real tornado went right by their porch. He could even add—as it howled and whirred, it lifted Grandpa and his rocker right off their porch and gave him the ride of his life. He really shouldn't forget to tell them that Grandpa landed safely down the road still smoking his pipe. Then again, Mrs. Hypo didn't like them to discuss anything dangerous or scary that really could happen. Gee, he was running out of ideas, and Mrs. Hypo would probably call on him anytime now.

Oh, he almost forgot—the time he rode the triple Ferris wheel that took him up, up, up into the sky, where he could look down and see the whole county fair. But then the class probably had been to Disneyland or that other place in Florida, where a triple Ferris wheel was just no big deal. His time was running out. Most of the class had shared something amazing, unusual, something he had never seen. What was he going to do? His hands began to sweat.

Then suddenly he had it. He remembered the time he went to the Safari Zoo, when he visited his grandmother. It was fun seeing all the animals he had read about: burly bears, oval pink ostriches, sassy seals, lecherous lions and very merry-go-lucky monkeys. There was a section on more uncommon animals. He had read about a baboon, a llama, a platypus, an anteater and even a caribou, but never a WOOSHY. And that was it—he was going to tell them what a wooshy was.

"Billy Martin," called Mrs. Hypo. "Billy Martin!"

"Oh, yes, Mrs. Hypo. Yes, I'm ready now." Billy, with his head down and his fists clenched, hanging by his side, began, "Well, ah, er, the most unusual thing I ever saw was a wooshy." Billy peeked his head up just enough to see what kind of a response he was getting.

"A wooshy?" yelled Bobby-know-it-all. "What's that?"

"I don't know," said Sarah. "Do you?"

"No, tell us," said the class.

Billy straightened his shoulders and lifted his head. His eyes shone brightly as he began, "Well I first saw a wooshy at the Safari Zoo. Of course I knew all the animals: a baboon, a llama, a platypus, an anteater and ever a caribou. Then in the last cage, I saw a most unusual creature called a wooshy. It looked . . . . (Describe it so the reader will be able to picture it in his/her mind.)

# The Peeper

# The Peeper

Sleep did not come easily to Mrs. Meyers this particular night. She was used to having few covers, because Mr. Meyers usually hogged them all. And she was used to little room, because Mr. Meyers hogged that too—he was a very big, burly kind of a man. But tonight there were more annoyances. As she wrestled for more covers, she kept hearing a very eerie sound, "P-E-E-P, peep-peep. P-E-E-P, peep-peep." She hit her slumbering husband on the head with a pillow and said, "George, stop making all those sounds. You must dreaming."

"That's not me," grumbled George, as he covered his head with the covers.

Mrs. Meyers sat upright in bed and pulled the covers off George's head and said, "Well, what is it? It's annoying."

"P-E-E-P, peep-peep. P-E-E-P, peep-peep."

"And rather strange."

George opened one eye and looked towards the window.
"It seems to be coming from out there. Just go out there and find out what it is."

"Oh, sure, just go out there and find out what it is," said Gertrude sarcastically," as George plopped back down in bed and covered his head with a pillow.

The old lady then pounced on him and said, "Get yourself out of that bed, George Meyers, and come with me. Did you ever think that something big and alive could go with that P-E-E-P, p-peeping, and eat me up?"

"Well, better you than me," said George.

"George, please!"

"OK, OK, just kidding. Let's go.

They both grabbed their matching terry cloth robes and went towards the door—Gertrude with club in hand, George with the flashlight. As they slowly proceeded toward the dense woods in back, they saw little flickers of light that seemed to bounce against the trees when the peeps sounded.

As they approached closer, closer, the peeping speeded up faster, faster. George whispered, "Maybe your curlers will scare it, Gertrude."

"This is not a time to be humorous, George."

"I was very serious and hopeful," he said.

They crouched behind a tree on the edge of the woods. They then poked their upper bodies around the tree and into the woods to have a peek. Mrs. Meyers had the bat over her head ready to attack—or throw and run. George was ready to turn on the flashlight. Peeping seemed to vacillate from tree to tree, and flickers of light were dancing merrily everywhere. The Meyers were ready; they were prepared; they were brave. F-L-A-S-H, the light went on. The peeping and dancing stopped. The flashlight blinked twice, and the light went out!

An eerie stillness crept into the air. The Meyers couldn't hear anything, but they could feel a strange soft wind blowing the hairs on their cheeks. Mrs. Meyers didn't dare move and felt like she had stopped breathing. The wind started to chill, and soon a little whirring noise was heard. Mrs. Meyers felt for George, but he had vanished! She clung to the tree as she whimpered and whispered, "George, George, where are you?"

She soon decided to crawl back to the house. Down on her hands and knees, she moved through the wet grass. All of a sudden her hand touched something that was blocking her way. She looked up as she heard, "P-E-E-P, peep-peep. P-E-E-P, peep-peep."

And this is what she saw. (Describe it so the reader will be able to picture it in his/her mind).

# Potato Head's Invention

# Potato Head's Invention

Potato Head was considered strange, weird, eccentric (anything but normal) by his eighth grade classmates at Boris High—but also very much a genius! He spent the first hour after each day of school skimming through pages in his school books absorbing and storing microscopic detail for future tests. When his brain felt somewhat appetized, he then went down to his dirty basement corner—filled with gadgets, wood, wires, unrecognizable parts and miscellaneous junk to his mother's dismay. To Potato Head it was a playpen for the intellectual curious, like himself.

In the past, the combination of Potato's mind and his playpen created some unusual, yet quite ingenious, inventions. He created a portable tree house; if you didn't like one tree, you could simply move it to another. He invented an expandable doghouse, one that grows with your dog. His go-cart can be navigated on water as well as land, and can fly across any obstacles in its way. Other interesting inventions were an indoor dog exerciser and a snow removal contraption.

His latest project remained a secret until the first baseball game of the season. He told everyone at school that he would change the world of baseball. It became the talk of Boris High. What was Potato Head's new invention: a 100 mile-an-hour ball or one that returns to the catcher, a mitt that guides the ball to it, some type of computer that can predict the outcome?

Everyone was waiting for Potato Head prior to the game. He was lugging what seemed to be a very heavy 4' x 4' cardboard box. As the school gathered around for the unveiling, Potato Head lifted the box. To everyone's amazement was Hip-or-Rah, a computerized fan. It looked like . . . . (Describe it so the reader will be able to picture it in his/her mind.)

# Unit III Characterization

# Introduction to Characterization

If you were asked to describe someone you knew, such as a mother or friend, you probably would list his/her character traits. Thoughtful, courteous and generous may come to mind. Or stingy, mean and bossy may apply. If you were asked how you decided upon these traits, you would give evidence by characters' actions and speech. The reader should go through the same process when making a decision with what a character in a story is like. He should be able to find supporting evidence of character traits by action and dialogue in the story.

Children, at a young age, can be taught to include characters' actions and speech in their writing. If not taught, what becomes a common occurrence is that the young writer will tell you what the main characters are like, "The witch was mean. The little boy was scared," and leave it at that with no action or dialogue. When this happens, the reader loses his visualization of a scene, and this leads to boredom. A reader envisions a scene by seeing the action and hearing dialogue. "The crooked-looking old witch laughed her hyena laugh as she sprinkled school-hating dust on the children." "The little boy was trembling so hard he couldn't move." The reader becomes more alert and in tune with what is happening in the story and interest is enhanced.

The art of giving characters action and dialogue is called characterization. Steps to enhance characterization are included in this chapter. They do not necessarily have to be taught in sequence.

1. Student exposure to the definition of characterization, action, dialogue and supporting evidence
2. Student exposure to characterization by identifying appropriate action in books and stories
3. Student exposure to characterization by identifying appropriate dialogue in books and stories
4. Student identifying/matching traits to action and dialogue
5. Student thinking of action and dialogue for character traits
6. Student exposure to various character traits
7. Student role-playing character traits with action and dialogue
8. Student applying characterization to his writing

# Cinderella and Little Red Riding Hood

Activity: Students read revised versions of "Cinderella" and "Little Red Riding Hood" by author and determine main character traits. They cite supporting evidence.

Materials: pages 65, 66, 67 and 68
pencil
other Cinderella or Little Red Riding Hood books and stories

Objectives:
1. Students will analyze stories for character traits.
2. Students will become familiar with the words *trait, dialogue, action* and *supporting evidence*.
3. Students will find examples of action and dialogue that support the trait they selected.
4. Students will see how characterization can change a story.

Directions: The teacher shares the following stories with class either by reading them or passing them out for students to read. After reading "Cinderella," the teacher asks what Cinderella was like. Answers should be similar to sad, kind, lonely, etc. The teacher then asks how you decided that. Students should then give supporting evidence (for example, she's always working; she has welled up tears). At this time it is appropriate for the teacher to explain the following terms: *trait, characterization, action, dialogue* and *supporting evidence*.

trait: what someone is like

characterization: giving a person action and/or dialogue to reinforce his/her character traits

action: what a character does

dialogue: what a person says

supporting evidence: something that gives you proof. For example, a person's actions and/or speech should give you proof that he has a certain trait or characteristic.

# Cinderella
## (Retold by Author)

"Would you please move, kitty? I must sweep this floor until it's spotless," said Cinderella as she swept the floor for the fourth time that very day. "Stepmother will be so angry, even if one crumb is left." Bookitty rubbed up against her as she knelt to the floor. Welled up tears drip-dropped to the floor. "Oh, Bookitty, what am I going to do? I want to go to the ball so badly, but I just have too much work to do. And just look at me—ragged clothes and full of soot."

Cinderella looked up as she heard, "Cinderella, Cinderella! Where are you, girl? Where's my ironed dress? Cinderella, do come here quick and fix my hair!" Cinderella hustled to her wicked stepsisters with ironed dress and curlers in hand.

Albertha bellowed, "'Bout time you got here. Now fix my hair! Hurry, hurry, we shan't be late for the Prince's big ball."

Matilda said, "Now clean up this mess while we are gone."

Cinderella hardly dared to whisper, "But I shall be at the ball, too."

"You, YOU? Give me a break. What would a pity-of-a-thing such as you do at a ball? Please, pray tell me." Then the two stepsisters roared with laughter.

"Sure, Cindie," anything you say," said Matilda. "But before you go, wash our clothes, make dinner for tomorrow, clean the dishes and oh, yes, start making our dresses for the next ball!"

"And Cindie, if by chance you should have time to even think about going to the ball, do look in the mirror first. Ha, ha, ha."

And the stepsisters departed to a world of gaiety, joy and laughter, leaving Cinderella to her world of dirt, sadness and tears.

Name _____

# Cinderella

A character *trait* describes what someone is like. A main character trait of Cinderella's in the story is _____.

The teacher will discuss answers with your class. You should be able to give examples from the story where she acted this way or what she did in the story. Write examples of her actions below.

_____
_____
_____
_____
_____
_____
_____

What character trait would you give to the stepsisters?

(Ask yourself what they were like.) _____

Sometimes instead of action, there will be examples of speech or dialogue that help explain what someone is like. Write dialogue below that explains the character trait you gave to them.

_____
_____
_____
_____
_____
_____
_____

So we now know that good writing includes character *action* and *dialogue* that help explain what they are like or their character trait(s). We call this art of giving character, their traits, *characterization*. Many future activities will familiarize you with this part of creative writing.

# Little Red Riding Hood
## (Retold by Author)

Once upon a time there was a sweet, loving wolf who lived in a wonderfully furnished carpeted woods. He was such a good father to all of his ten wooflets, but he had a hard time making enough money to feed them all. So one day he decided to go visit Old Lady Gramma to see if he could work for her. He was willing to do anything—cut logs, hunt, clean, cook. He just wanted to be a good father and provide for his children.

He knocked and he knocked at her door, but no one answered. He finally went inside to see if she was all right—the kind wolf that he was. Gramma wasn't around, so he decided to wait for her. He waited and waited. He began yawning, because he was getting very tired. He saw some jammies hanging on a hook. Thinking he'd just take a little nap, he put them on, and soon was fast asleep in Gramma's bed.

Hearing a knock, knock, knock, he awoke. In walked a little red-riding-hooded girl looking for Gramma. "Gramma, where are you? I have some bread in my basket for you." The wolf didn't want to scare her (he heard little girls were afraid of wolves), so he decided to pretend he was Gramma. The little girl came up to Gramma and said, "Why Gramma, I'm so sorry you are ill. You must be very sick, because you don't look like yourself at all. My what big eyes you have?" said Little Red.

"The better to see you with," blinked the wolf.

"My what a big mouth you have?"

The better to eat your bread with," smiled the fanged wolf.

"Well, I'll just get you some." The wolf leaned over to look in the basket to see what she had and his granny cap fell off.

"Why, why you aren't Gramma at all!" cried Little Red. "You're a mean, nasty, lying wolf. We will send you to jail for this."

As the story goes, sirens wailed and in came three blue-uniformed policemen with big billy clubs. They knocked him on the head, handcuffed him and began dragging him out the door.

However, just in the nick of time, in walks Gramma and reads the note the wolf wrote. "In case I fall asleep, I just want some work, so I can feed my family. Wolf"

She puts down the note and says, "Oh, you poor wolf. I would like to hire you to protect me from burglars."

So the wolf lived happily ever after—taking care of Gramma and his family. And, of course, he even forgave Little Red, being the kind wolf that he was.

Name _____

# Little Red Riding Hood

1. In most "Little Red Riding Hood" stories the wolf is mean. This author insists the wolf is kind. The author will be believable if there are examples of his kindness. Write down some examples below. Be prepared to discuss with the class.

   _____
   _____
   _____
   _____
   _____
   _____

2. Are there any other characteristics you'd give the wolf? Give examples that would support your answers.

   _____
   _____
   _____
   _____
   _____
   _____

3. Compare this Little Red Riding Hood with another one where the wolf was mean. Give examples of the other wolf's meanness.

   _____
   _____
   _____
   _____
   _____
   _____

4. Rewrite your own fairy tales, changing character traits. Some suggestions:
   Mean Three Little Pigs and kind Wolf
   Vain Snow White
   Lazy Cinderella
   Curious Three Little Bears and timid Goldilocks
   Honest Pinocchio and dishonest Geppetto

Name _____

# Character Research

Directions: Find examples of either the character's action or dialogue that supports his/her character trait.

1. Morris is *finicky* because _____
   _____

2. Alice (in *Alice in Wonderland*) is *curious* because _____
   _____

3. Scrooge is *stingy* because _____
   _____

4. Caddie Woodlawn is *brave* because _____
   _____

5. Tom Sawyer is *adventurous* because _____
   _____

6. Heidi is *kind* because _____
   _____

Now find your own favorite character's traits and supporting evidence.

7. _____
   _____

8. _____
   _____

9. _____
   _____

10. _____
    _____

# A Ride to the Beach

Activity: After reading "A Ride to the Beach" on page 71, students decide on the main character trait of each girl and give supporting evidence.

Materials: page 71
paper to record data (optional)

Objectives: 1. Students will analyze story for character traits.
2. Students will find examples of dialogue that support the trait they selected.

Directions: The teacher may choose to either pass "A Ride to the Beach" out to students or read it to them. After reading it, students should be able to describe a strong character trait for each girl. The teacher should lead the class in a discussion of why they chose certain character traits for each girl. "Well, Sue Ann is pessimistic because she says it is going to rain, and Amy's boyfriend is going to look at other girls." To lend depth to this assignment, the teacher may direct students to record data supporting character traits. Students should come up with answers similar to the following:

Melissa: optimistic
Sue Ann: pessimistic
Laurie: daydreamer, romanticist
Amy: in love, jealous, possessive

# A Ride to the Beach

Directions: Read the dialogue of four teenage girls driving to the beach. Describe a strong character trait for each girl by the end of the conversation.

Melissa: "Oh, aren't we lucky to be going to the beach? The sun is going to shine through, and we'll have a great day!"

Sue Ann: "I don't think so. It looks like it's going to rain any minute. Maybe we better turn around."

Melissa: "Well, even if it rains, it's great getting away from town. We can go in the little fun shops nearby. Anyway, I bet the sun shines a good part of the day."

Sue Ann: "I bet it doesn't. Well, I hope there will be enough food to eat."

Melissa: "There should be. Everyone seems to have brought plenty. I know I brought lots of sandwiches."

Sue Ann: "Do you think they'll spoil?"

Laurie: (has been looking out the window all this time—kind of dreamy-eyed) "I'm sorry, what did you say?"

Sue Ann: "Never mind."

Laurie: "Oh, I'm going to meet Mr. Wonderful today. I just know it. Oh, look at that cloud. It reminds me of a wonderfully soft bed. Ah-h-h it feels so good. Oh, where am I? Ah, yes, I'm in Florida, where the boys are."

Amy: "I wonder what Tom is doing? He sure is wonderful. He's probably making a triple decker sandwich special right now. I hope he's not waiting on a girl."

Melissa: "Oh don't worry about him. There will be lots of boys at the beach."

Sue Ann: "Oh sure there will be."

Amy: "I don't care about any other boys. Just Tom. Anyway I told him I wouldn't look at any other boys. That way he won't look at any girls."

Sue Ann: "Yes, he will! Boys will be boys.

Melissa: "Stop that, Sue Ann. Are we going to have a good time today or not?"

Laurie: "Did someone say *good time*? I'm ready. I'm ready to float on a raft and just have that sun tan me while I think of warm thoughts."

Sue Ann: "Warm? I think it's getting cold."

Amy: "I miss Tom."

# Character Traits

Activity: Up to this point, students have found examples of dialogue and action supporting a particular trait. Now they will be thinking/writing their own action and dialogue for a particular character trait.

Materials: pages 73, 74 and 75
paper and pencil
writing notebook to take notes from observing real character traits (optional)

Objectives:
1. Students will become familiar with over fifty character traits.
2. Students will become more aware of appropriate dialogue and action for certain character traits.
3. Students will write appropriate action for character traits.
4. Students will write appropriate dialogue for character traits.

Directions:
1. The teacher reviews character traits with students. Teacher may review by asking what certain characters were like.
2. The class brainstorms a list of character traits similar to page 73.
3. The teacher either provides students with their own brainstormed list or the one on page 73 as a resource.
4. Teacher assigns page 74 on a kind student. The class may observe such action and dialogue for a few days and write their observations. A notebook would be very appropriate here. The same assignment for all students will illustrate to students various possible responses reflecting the same trait and help students feel more comfortable with the following assignment.
5. Students should share responses on page 74. When students have mastered this to the teacher's satisfaction, they are ready for page 75.
6. The teacher assigns page 75.
7. Again, responses need to be shared and discussed.
8. From this point onward, characterization should be a part of the students' writing.

# Character Traits

| | | | |
|---|---|---|---|
| shy | optimistic | creative | ambitious |
| studious | nervous | pessimistic | sensible |
| lazy | romantic | scared | humorous |
| lonely | contented | serious | adventurous |
| bold | proud | introverted | worried |
| mean | sassy | courteous | sensitive |
| extroverted | kind | sarcastic | sympathetic |
| snobby | selfish | gregarious | respectful |
| generous | calm | brave | unselfish |
| snoopy | smart | energetic | disrespectful |
| cheap | careful | careless | vain |
| clumsy | jealous | friendly | perfectionistic |
| sickly | humble | domestic | rebellious |
| emotional | sentimental | lovesick | athletic |

**One who is a:**

| | | | |
|---|---|---|---|
| bragger | flirt | apple polisher | leader |
| follower | class clown | animal lover | risk taker |
| claustrophobic | jock | sports enthusiast | liar |

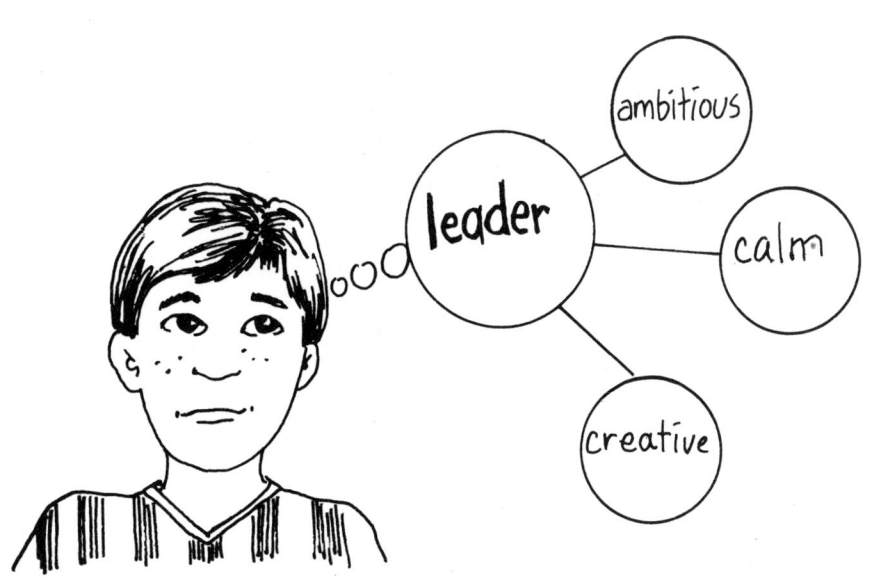

Name _____

# Characterization Work Sheet

1. List things a kind student would say?

   _____
   _____
   _____
   _____
   _____
   _____
   _____
   _____

2. List things (actions) a kind student would do?

   _____
   _____
   _____
   _____
   _____
   _____
   _____
   _____

3. Write a scene about a kind student and a new student having trouble adjusting to school. Use some of your examples above in your scene.

   _____
   _____
   _____
   _____
   _____
   _____
   _____
   _____

Name _____

# Characterization Work Sheet

1. List a character trait from page 73. _____

2. List things this kind of person would do (action).

   _____
   _____
   _____
   _____
   _____
   _____
   _____

3. List things this kind of person would say (dialogue).

   _____
   _____
   _____
   _____
   _____
   _____
   _____

4. Read to the class and have other students guess what kind of person you are describing.

5. Write a story about the kind of person you described. Include some of your actions and dialogue.

# Characters

Activity: Students will identify characters' actions and dialogue in the game Characters.

Materials: directions to game on page 80
characterization cards on pages 77-79 copied and cut out. May choose to put on heavier board and laminate.
box or container to house game

Objectives: 
1. Students will identify characters' actions and dialogue.
2. Students will become aware that we need action and dialogue in writing.
3. Students will become more aware of possible character traits.

Directions: Refer to page 80 for specific step-by-step directions. The teacher may choose to guide students through the directions.

Cut and make into cards.

| | | |
|---|---|---|
| **SMART MARY** | Mary finished first in the spelling bee again this year. | "I would like the extra challenge, Miss Brown, since I'm done with all of my schoolwork." |
| **SHY SUSAN** | She blushed when the teacher called on her. Then she hung her head and whispered the answer to the floor. | "I would prefer not to give a speech in front of the whole class. Could I please tape it?" |
| **BOSSY MATILDA** | She told them that they were doing wrong with each of their dance steps. | "Debby, you'll be first. Jenny will be second. Then I will decide who will be third." |
| **KIND MR. GRANT** | He helped the cat down from the tree. | "May I help you with that, Mrs. Jones?" |

Cut and make into cards.

| TATTLETALE MARK | He came running in from the playground to tell his teacher someone was saying he had cooties. | "Mr. Baker, Erik took cuts getting a drink . . . and Brandy won't give me my place back in line . . . and . . ." |
|---|---|---|
| MEAN OLD MRS. OLSON | She threw her scrawny arms in the air with a rake, because someone stepped on her precious property. | "I don't believe in Halloween, so you don't get any candy." SLAM! |
| DAREDEVIL DERIK | He threw the ball towards Mrs. Olson's window to see how close he could come without really hitting it. "Oh, oh." | "I challenge you to stand on your head underwater till you see a fish swim by." |
| MESSY MELISSA | First a spaghetti noodle fell to her skirt. Then a piece of lettuce glued itself to her arm, and then a clump of pudding made it all the way down to the tip of her shoe. | "Mom, I don't know why I should clean my room; it will just get dirty again. However, I do need to find some clothes to wear." |

Cut and make into cards.

| | | |
|---|---|---|
| **APPLE-POLISHER PENNY** | She straightened the teacher's desk during recess and then sat at her desk smiling from ear to ear when the teacher walked in. | "Mrs. Green, you are the best teacher in the whole world. May I sit next to Jennifer?" |
| **CRY BABY CARRIE** | She went bawling to her mother just because she skinned her knee, and it didn't even bleed. | "Sniffle, sniffle. I need help on this problem and no-o-o-o one will help me. Sniffle, sniffle." |
| **BULLY BEN** | He gave two kids a black eye in one week. | "If you don't get out of my way, I'll run you over." |
| **ENERGETIC EARNEY** | After he washed the car and mowed the lawn, he painted the garage. | With his friends huffing and puffing in the background, he said, "Oh, come on you guys, we can run another ten minutes." |

# Characters

Materials: two to four players
character cards
paper for keeping score

Objective: To acquire the most sets of character cards. A set includes a dialogue card, an action card and related character card. The winner at the end of the game is the one with the most sets.

## Steps of Play

1. All materials are set up for play. It doesn't matter who goes first. Two to four players may play.
2. The dealer passes out six cards to each player. The rest of the cards are placed facedown in a pile.
3. Players look at cards and try to match sets. A set includes a related dialogue card, action card and character card.
4. First player either draws from pile or from opponent's hand. If he picks from opponent's hand, opponent may draw from pile. Player must discard. If he has a matching set, he may lay his set down and get another turn. Second player either draws from pile or from opponent's hand. If he has a matching set, he may lay his set down and get another turn.
5. A player may opt to pick up all of the discarded pile during his play, remembering all cards in his hand at end of game are subtracted from game points. Three cards in hand are subtracted from three cards laid down.
6. Game continues until someone is out of cards. Winner is the one with the most points. Every card laid down is a point, so a set would be 3 points. Every card left in hand is a point. Number of points left in hand is subtracted from number of points laid down.

## Game Options

1. Player may ask opponent for a certain card. If opponent has it, he must hand it over and draw from the pile.
2. Play may continue until everyone is out of cards.
3. Player may place two cards down at a time instead of three. However opponent could place the related set card down to get a point.
4. Game may continue until someone reaches a set score. So there may be several games within a game.

Index cards are given to each player.

# Characterization: Role Playing

Activity: Students act out characters and the class decides on their character traits based on action and dialogue.

Materials: envelopes with scene descriptions on pages 83-87
cards with character traits on pages 83-87
   (All character cards should be in appropriate matching scene envelope.)
space for acting
student actors
props if desired (for example, plate for cafeteria scene)

Objective: Students will be encouraged to use action and dialogue when they write about characters, because it will help to create more visual scenes for the reader and actually place him there. It is also helpful if the writer can visualize himself as a part of the scene when developing a character.

Directions: Four students are each given a card, with a character description on each. They are to become that personality in the role-playing situation given them. The class guesses their personality by their actions and dialogue. Examples: Amy is shy: she spoke softly and looked down often. Fred is careless: he handed his paper in quickly and didn't recheck it. He said, "I don't want to take the time." Those actions and dialogue that convinced students of the particular personality should be discussed afterwards. The same approach is used in stories and books.

It should also be related how action and dialogue should be included in writing. Once the author decides what a character is like, he or she can brainstorm how the character would talk and act and include it in his writing.

# Role-Playing Situations

Scene 1: Miss Jones is the teacher trying to conduct a class session. Four students will be taking a spelling test. She begins by asking them to put everything away, hand in the written assignment and get out paper for taking the test.

Character Traits: (Should be put on index cards and given to actors individually.)

Miss Jones: (Students do not guess this person. It is just to help the scene.) This role-playing scene works best if the real teacher plays the teacher. The teacher may want to begin by stating: "Class, please put everything away as you turn in your writing assignment. Now get out some paper for taking your spelling test."

Teacher may use the words following or make up his/her own:
1. relief
2. sought
3. inspection
4. vitamin
5. energetic
6. cherish
7. aspire

Student One: You are a conscientious, serious student who likes things to go smoothly.

Student Two: You are a very unprepared, disorganized student.

Student Three: You are the teacher's pet, a true apple-polisher.

Student Four: You are disrespectful and the class clown.

Scene 2: A group of business people get on an elevator. They get in on the first floor. They all push buttons to upper floors. The elevator goes to the second floor. It then goes upward towards the third floor. All of a sudden the elevator begins vibrating violently. Then BANG, BANG and the elevator drops a foot knocking everyone down to the floor. Passengers (actors) slowly get up realizing they are stuck between the second and third floors. Acting begins.

Character Traits: (Should be put on index cards and given to actors individually.)

Businessman One: You are a claustrophobic (cannot stand to be closed or locked in). You really panic. You were on your way to see a psychiatrist.

Businessman Two: You are a workaholic (a constant worker, who doesn't do anything but work). You were on your way to an important business meeting that is to begin in five minutes.

Businessman Three: You are a public leader who is very considerate of the feelings of others. You feel better about yourself when other people feel good. You were on your way to a board meeting to donate some money to help the handicapped.

Businessman Four: You are a very calm and collected person. You know how to keep your cool even under the most difficult conditions. You were on your way to the spa to join some friends in a hot tub.

Scene 3: Two teenage girls are sitting in a booth in a hamburger joint, which is the school hangout. Two teenage boys come into the restaurant. One is a cool-looking dude, another—a nerd. They ask to join the girls because there appears to be no other seats available.

Character Traits: (Should be put on index cards and given to actors individually.)

Girl One: You are boy crazy and are impressed with good looks.

Girl Two: You are very shy, and you embarrass easily.

Boy One: You are very handsome, confident and a class leader.

Boy Two: You are a boring bore and a genius. You are very uncomfortable around girls even though you sincerely like them.

Scene 4: Four girls—Amy, Lisa, Kim and Susan—meet while walking to school. They walk the rest of the way to school together. Kim is wearing brand-new designer jeans. Amy also has jeans on, that is jeans from K Mart. The subject of jeans turns out to be the main conversation. The other girls have jeans on also but not designer.

Character Traits: (Should be put on index cards and given to actors individually.)

Amy: You are self-conscious and sensitive. It really bothers you if anyone notices anything wrong with you.

Kim: You are a bragger and conceited. You are always trying to outdo people.

Susan: You are very jealous of other people and what they have.

Lisa: You are very secure with who you are. You aren't bothered if someone has something that you don't.

Scene 5: Two couples, the Hanks and the Breens, have begun vacationing on a cruise ship. The Hanks and the Breens, never meeting before, have been seated together at the same dinner table. They all try to enjoy a wonderful meal of lobster and steak.

Character: (Should be put on index cards and given to actors individually.)
Traits:
Mr. Hanks: You are somewhat poor mannered and selfish. You care only about feeding your own face.

Mrs. Hanks: You are overly embarrassed and apologetic. Your husband's poor manners are a disgrace to you.

Mr. Breen: You are a jokester. You try to make the best out of any situation.

Mrs. Breen: You are polite and courteous. You don't get upset easily.

Scene 6: Four workers are seen finishing cars that have just gone through the machine-washing part of a car wash. This particular crew of men handles hosing down mats, vacuuming the inside and wiping them down to a shine.

Character (Should be put on index cards and given to actors individually.)
Traits:
Pete: You are an ambitious, goal-oriented, hard worker. You want the boss to notice so you'll be promoted.

Joe: You are lazy and try to get away with as little as possible. Since the other guys are willing to work so hard, you think you can slack off and the boss won't notice.

Tom: You are creative and try to think of things to make life better. You're just a happy person.

Chris: You are very bored. You want to do a good job, but this must be the 298th car you've worked on today.

Scene 7: This is the first day in an apartment which four roommates have just moved into.

Character Traits: (Should be put on index cards and given to actors individually.)

Roommate One: You are a very neat person. You can't stand any dirt or clutter. You are also very organized.

Roommate Two: You are sloppy, careless, messy and unorganized.

Roommate Three: You are bossy and domineering.

Roommate Four: You are easygoing. Things just don't bother you too much.

Scene 8: This takes place in a school cafeteria. Student One goes through the lunch line and gets his/her lunch. The rest of the characters have already been seated and are eating. Student One finishes getting her lunch and starts to go toward their table. She then drops her lunch IN FRONT OF EVERYBODY!

Character Traits: (Should be put on index cards, and given to actors individually.)

Student One: You are very shy, self-conscious and overly sensitive. You think you're going to die over spilling lunch IN FRONT OF EVERYBODY!

Student Two: You are a mean bully. You enjoy making jokes over others' miseries.

Student Three: You are a sympathetic, caring person, who tries to make people feel more comfortable over embarrassing moments.

Student Four: You are unsympathetic and uncaring. You feel people cause their own problems, and you would never think to help someone out.

# Unit IV Plot Development

It was the most miserable day in my ten-year-old life: from a cold shower to a miserable breakfast to . . . .

At that moment I should have gotten back into bed with pneumonia symptoms. But being the trouper I am, I dressed and went down for some warm breakfast. Cold oatmeal and hard, nonbuttered toast greeted me. Todd had just gotten sick all over his high chair tray. I gnawed on my toast as my mother kept repeating, "Hurry up or you're going to miss your bus, and as you can see, I don't have time to take you to school."

# Introduction to Plot

The author feels working with the devleopment of plots should never be ignored in creative writing, because it lends structure to one's writing. Once plot is decided upon, the writer knows where he is going and has a basis where to start. Often student writers can't get off the ground with their writing, because they are either uncomfortable with a specific assignment to write on, or they can't come up with an idea if assigned to write on any topic of their own choosing. Other students get off the ground and can write and write, but it may lead into one tangent after another. Many of these necessary loopholes for the young writer may be avoided if time is spent with plot development prior to writing stories.

Several tools to help students with plot development are included in this chapter. First to get students' writing off the ground, a resource of 100 plot ideas has been provided. To aid students in generating their own ideas is a plot category list to be used with webbing, explained further in this chapter.

Once the student has a general idea for his plot, generated from above, a mini plot should be developed. In most cases this includes the main character or characters, setting, goals, and obstacles getting in the way of the goals. How the story is resolved and some sequencing of events may also be included. This should be designed prior to the writer's story writing to keep the writer always in touch with where he is going with his writing. This can be a tremendous aid in alleviating students' rambling on about unimportant things in the story.

Several lessons have been provided on mini plots. The first one introduces students to the main ingredients of a plot. Then in a fun way, students can make up hundreds of character-setting-goal-obstacle combinations. Then they write mini plots and develop them into stories.

Eleven mini plots have been developed for students to write from. This gives students a good example of what should be done prior to writing; they'll see how much easier it is to write a story; and they can compare their stories to others who have written on the same plot.

The chapter concludes with a developed story from one of the mini plots. It may be used as a resource and for analysis.

# Plot Generating

Activity: Given a list of plot ideas, students will develop stories. Given different categories for plots, students will develop plot ideas and eventually stories.

Materials: writing materials (paper and pencils)
plot resource sheets, pages 92-94
plot webs, pages 96-99
magazines, short stories, children's books (optional)

Objectives: 1. Students will find areas of interest they feel comfortable about writing on.
2. Students will not have an excuse that they can't think of anything to write about.
3. Students will have an available resource of ideas, which they can draw upon at any time.
4. Students will become familiar with plot themes and categories.
5. Students will learn to design a story around their own interests and work out the specifics.

Directions: The following pages on plot ideas may be used in several ways. The resource sheets may be used simply any time students need a story idea to write on, allowing for the inclusion of their own ideas. However, experience of coming up with their own ideas (with guidance) should even more assure that they pick an idea they are familiar and comfortable with. The following pages on webbing give them categories to begin their thinking. Students look through the categories and find ones of interest. The teacher asks for additions. As a warm-up, students may discuss stories they have read in certain categories. Again, the resource sheets will provide examples of what plot ideas are.

First, all students should be assigned the same webbing sheet (summer vacation) and share their examples. This will make students feel more comfortable with doing one on their own.

If students have trouble getting started, the teacher may try some prompting as the following:

"What things make up this category?"
"What kinds of things can happen in this category?"
"Where is there *conflict* in this category?"

If a student all of a sudden gets excited about a plot, it is suggested he be allowed to either begin his story or jot down ideas. Webbing may be used for this purpose, also. Take a webbing sheet and make the center the plot idea; the circles around become ideas to include in the story, which may lead to sequential steps in the story. (See Unit V.)

*Conflict is a situation in the story that needs resolving.

# 100 Plot Ideas
## Pets

1. The stray I couldn't keep
2. The stray who adopted me
3. The funniest/naughtiest cat I ever owned
4. The house with a cat, a dog and a canary
5. Bowser is just too big for his house.
6. We finally can have a pet.
7. A job in a pet shop
8. You may pick either the dog or the cat, but one has to go
9. The city overrun with cats
10. Baby calves grow up, Brandon, so be prepared!
11. The three-legged dog
12. Bandit's search for his lost family
13. The cat who loved dogs
14. 597 guppies, more to come, and I can't kill one.
15. Our farm, the dumping ground for all homeless and injured animals

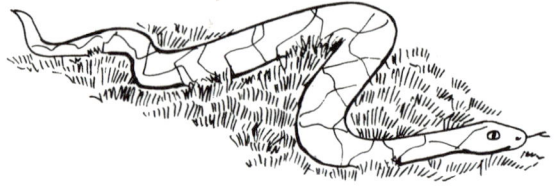

## Other Animals

16. The day the monkey got hold of the keys
17. A boa got loose and can't be found.
18. The kittens found a home in the zoo.
19. Alma the baboon is unhappy because he doesn't have a friend at the zoo.
20. They want to tear the city zoo down.
21. Saving the oil-covered ducks
22. How the camel really got its hump
23. The animal's great escape from the plane's cargo
24. The town's fight to save only a whale
25. A fawn's new life after fire took everything away
26. How all the forest animals get together and save their land
27. I've become a vegetarian because . . . .
28. Wild horses are eating up all our land.
29. How to save the last manatee in the world
30. The world discovers a new pet that is cuddly, housebroken, can get its own food, doesn't smell and is a great protector.

## Sports

31. The one-armed pitcher
32. The girl who dreamed to be on the hockey team
33. The football star who didn't want to play football
34. The skiing champ who lost her leg
35. Creston's team gets laughed off the field for the last time!
36. Silverton, you just have to win the Kentucky Derby.
37. So big deal, you're the best skateboard rider in the world.
38. I'm in love with my tennis instructor.
39. My dad is our new coach, but he can't coach.
40. The coach and I just don't see eye to eye.

## Family

41. If Susan borrows my clothes one more time, . . .
42. The day Dad walked out of our lives
43. Too many kids and not enough food
44. We're getting a sister from India.
45. Home on the streets
46. I have to live with a retarded brother.
47. Mom decides to start working.
48. The day Mom and Dad stopped spoiling us
49. What are we ever going to do with Grandpa, the grump?
50. Baby brother brat gets all the attention.

## Space

51. The big move to space
52. My friend, the alien
53. Do you think Herbert could be an alien?
54. A new world discovered!
55. The space war is on.
56. My accidental step into space
57. How to trap an alien
58. Now that I am on Mars, Mom, can you come and get me?
59. The Martians are here!
60. Life, growing up in space

# School

61. Classroom hero
62. Teacher's leaving
63. Lucky me; I got the teacher no one wanted.
64. Am I good at anything, teacher? Please tell me.
65. I hate math, and it hates me.
66. How the new principal turned around our school
67. The school pact to do away with homework
68. How this "flunkie" coped
69. What it is like to go to Briarwood Snobby Junior High
70. Yes, teacher, I live in a car, but please don't tell anyone.

# Growing Up

71. Your first job
72. Your first love
73. No girls allowed in our club
74. How I turned Miss Prep
75. I'm in love with my next door neighbor.
76. I never fit in anywhere.
77. My steps to winning Jenny's attention
78. I was so embarrassed I thought I'd die.
79. Just saying no isn't always so easy.
80. I didn't have problems till my pimples sprouted.

81. My best friend and I like the same guy, but she doesn't know it.
82. Being smart isn't easy in Harlem.
83. My boyfriend got Snow King and I got nothing.
84. Holding down two jobs just to keep up with my friends
85. My parents just don't understand what it's like to be a teenager.
86. Stealing my girlfriend back
87. The year I grew up
88. So what if I don't get all A's, B's or C's.
89. It's tough being the tallest girl in seventh grade.
90. I'll do anything for Miss Thomas.
91. The only one not invited to the party
92. How my enemy became my friend
93. There's got to be a way to get into the IN crowd.
94. If I become friends with Ben, then Jeremy won't be my friend
95. Five best friends forever
96. My two best friends died, and I can't go on.
97. New school and no new friends
98. Our plan to get everyone not to like Bobby Sue
99. Being a soccer star just isn't important in this neighborhood.
100. I can get along without friends; no problem!

# Plot Categories

Directions: Select a category below or think of one yourself to be used with plot webbing on page 99.

Animals
  alligators
  bears
  beavers
  cows
  elephants
  hippos
  horses
  monkeys
  snakes
Business
Cars
Camp
City life
Country life
Computers
Crime
Dinosaurs
Dragons
Family
Farming
Fashion
Fighting
Food
Friends
Future
Government
Growing up
Halloween
Haunted house
Heroes
History
Hobbies
Holidays

Hospital life
Island life
Jobs
  detective
  doctor
  fireman
  salesman
  teacher
  veterinarian
Magic
Medical
  accidents
  diseases
  injured
  medicine
  sickness
Misfortunates
Monsters
Movie stars
Murders
Music
Natural disasters
  earthquake
  flood
  hurricane
  tornado
Neighbors
Old people
Other lands
Parties
Places
Poverty
Rainy days
Ranching

Religion
Robbery
Royalty
School
  nursery
  preschool
  elementary
  high school
  college
Science
Seaside
Shopping
Snowy days
Space
Sports
  baseball
  basketball
  boating
  football
  golf
  hockey
  Olympics
  pool
  racing
  soccer
  tennis
Supermarket
Travel
Vacations
Video games
Valentine's Day
War
White House
Wizardry
World events/problems

# Plot Webs

Directions: After reading over the resource sheets of 100 Plot Ideas, you still may not have found one to your liking or you may just prefer to think of one yourself. A good place to start is to think of an area of interest to you. You may find the plot category list on page 95 helpful to you. Once you find an area of interest, write it in the center of the web in the rectangle. If summer vacation was of interest to you, you'd write it as below.

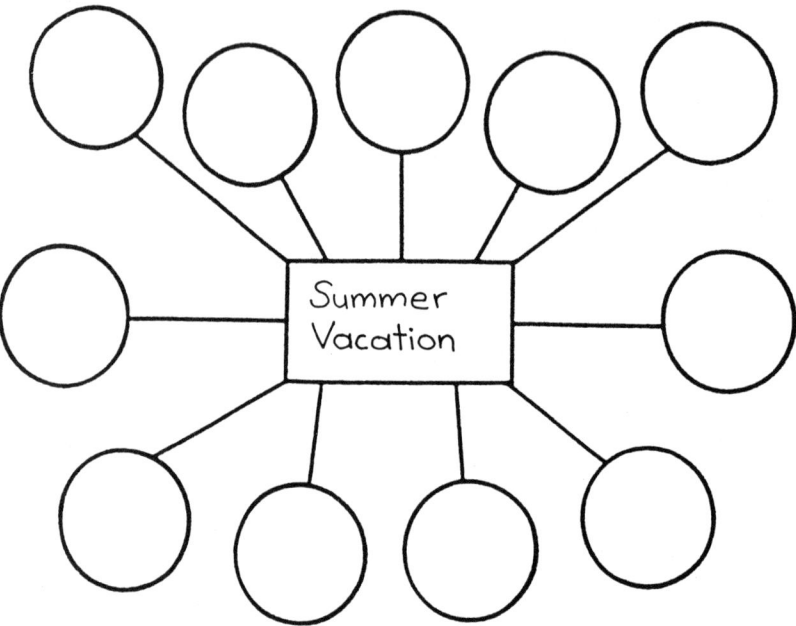

Then begin thinking about kinds of things that happen during this time that would make good stories. Try to think of things where there is a problem or conflict in the story that has to be worked out. As you get ideas, write them in the circles. When your circles are full of ideas, you should be able to select one you feel comfortable to write on.

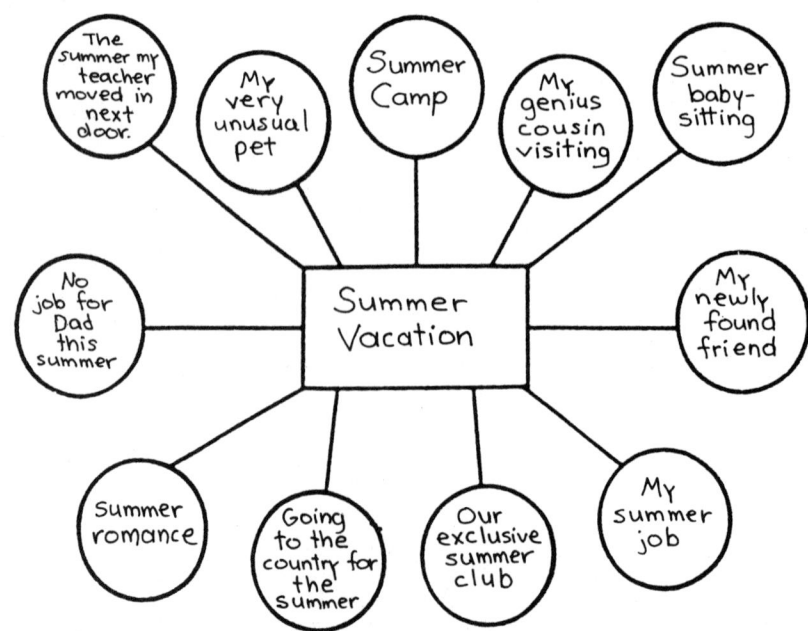

Name _____

**Directions:** Think about the topic in the middle of the web and related ideas that could make good stories. Write your brainstormed ideas in the circles. When your circles are filled up, select one, and develop it into a story.

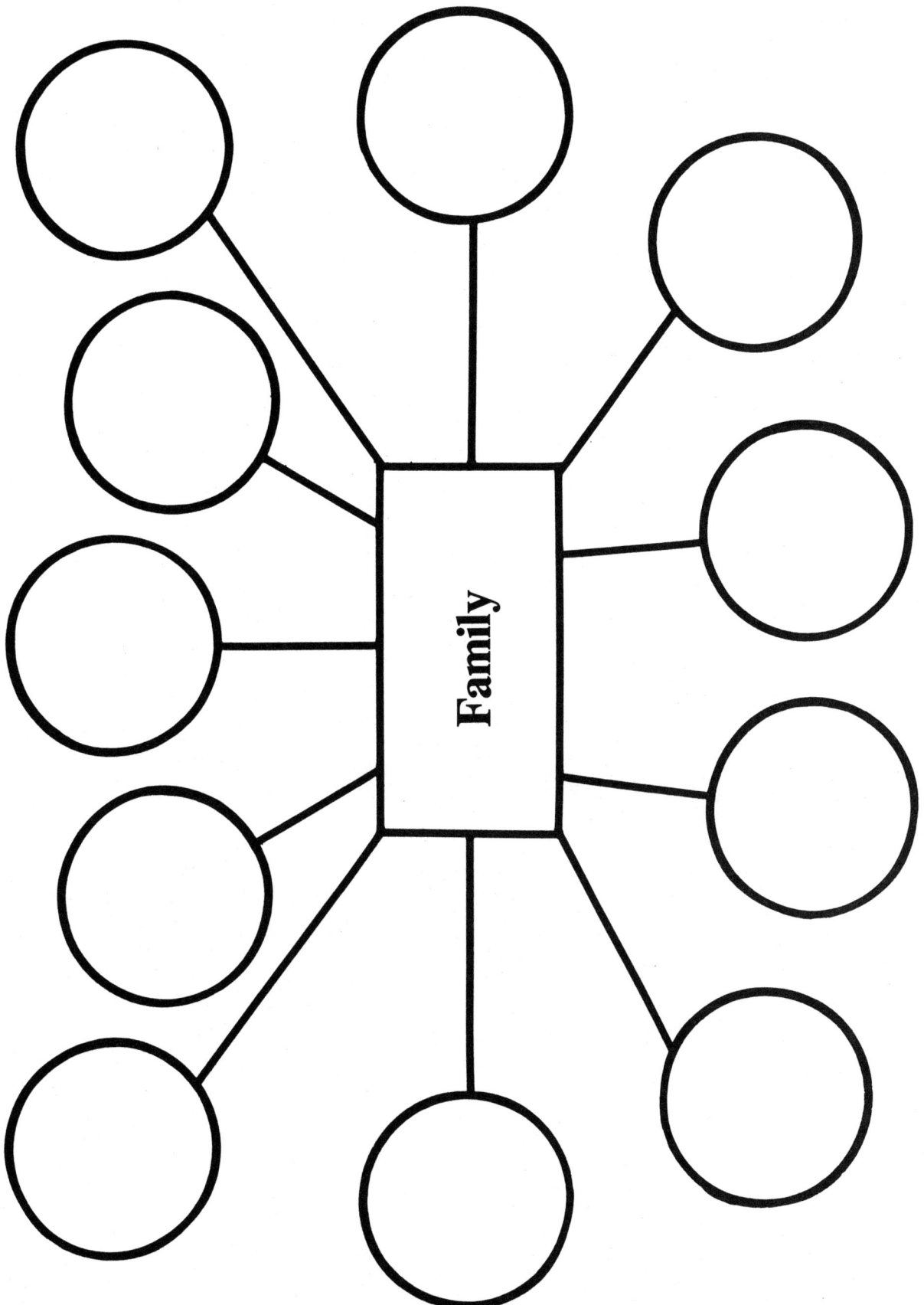

Name _____

Directions: Think about the topic in the middle of the web and related ideas that could make good stories. Write your brainstormed ideas in the circles. When your circles are filled up, select one, and develop it into a story.

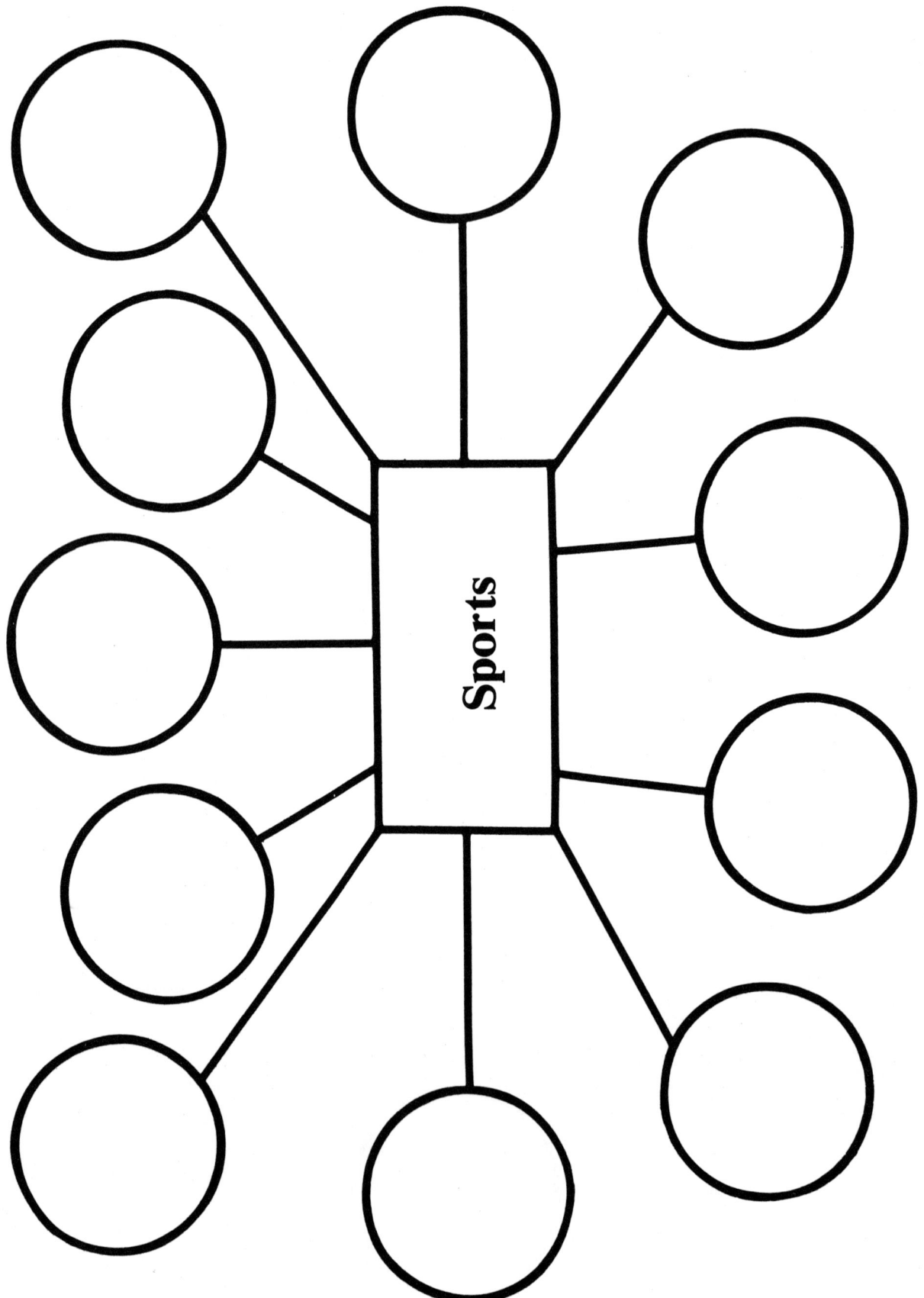

Copyright © 1990, Good Apple, Inc.

Name _____

**Directions:** Write a topic of interest to you in the middle rectangle. Write your brainstormed ideas about the topic for stories in the circles. When your circles are filled up, select one and develop it into a story.

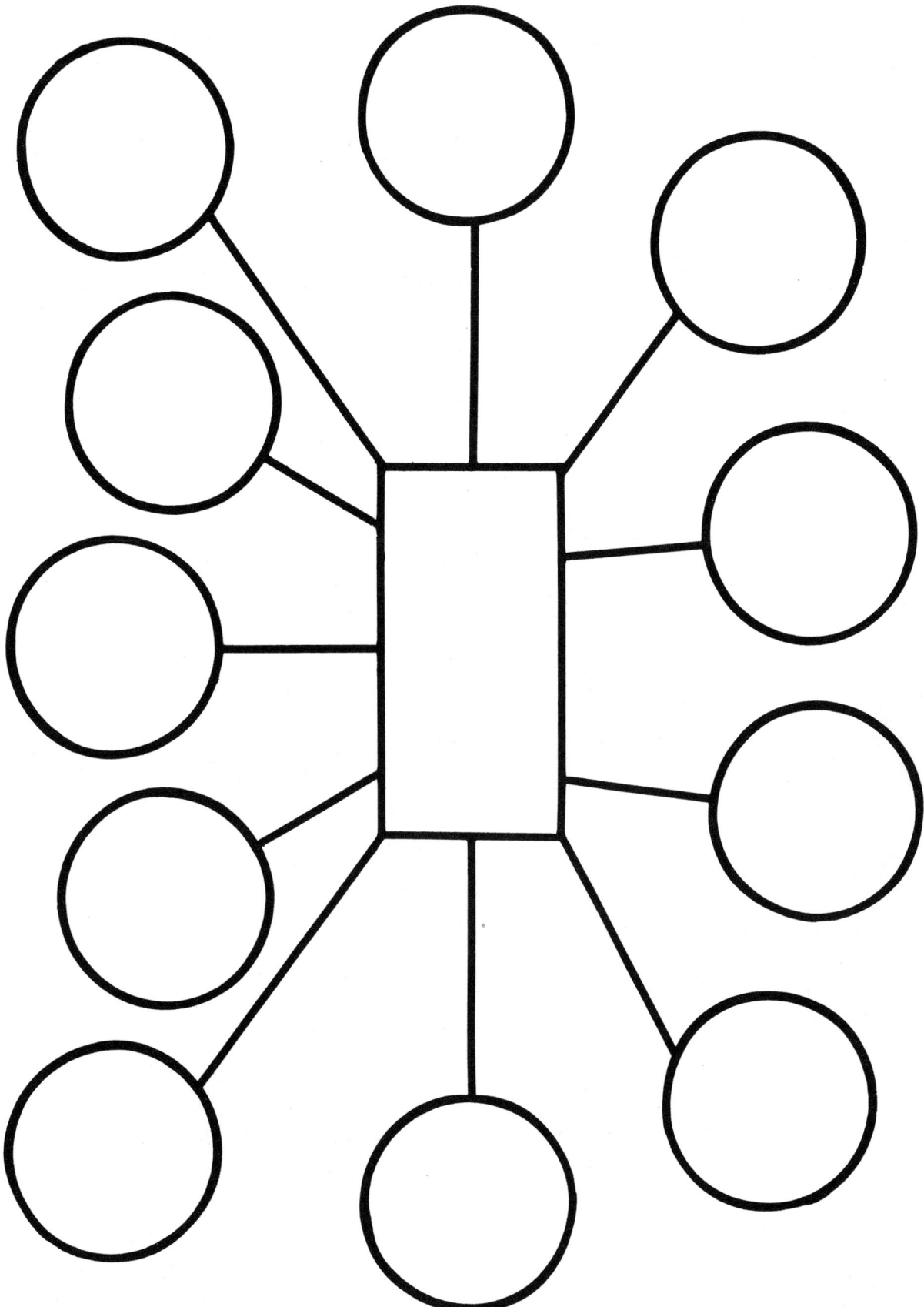

# Plot Grid

Activity: Given the main character, setting, goal and obstacle of a story, the student will design a mini plot. He then may develop it into a story.

Materials: writing materials (writing paper, pencils)
page 103 enlarged to poster size
48 cards made from page 104

Objectives:
1. Students will learn about the four ingredients of a plot.
2. Students will learn how one ingredient in a plot can change the whole story.
3. Students will have to creatively design a plot around four (may be unrelated) ingredients.
4. Students will become aware of the structure of a plot.
5. Students will not have to worry about getting over the hump of designing a plot before they write.

Directions: Teacher enlarges the plot grid on page 103 to poster size or larger to be displayed in front of room for instruction. During instruction, she explains that the four main parts of a story are the characters, setting, goals of the character(s) and obstacles. The obstacles create the conflict or problem in a story that needs to be resolved. The teacher may choose to expand on this depending upon the needs of the students.

Next the teacher shares the grid made up of ideas for the four parts of a story. The grid may be used in various ways (student selection, teacher selection or random selection). The author suggests to start with random selection which should give interesting and humorous results.

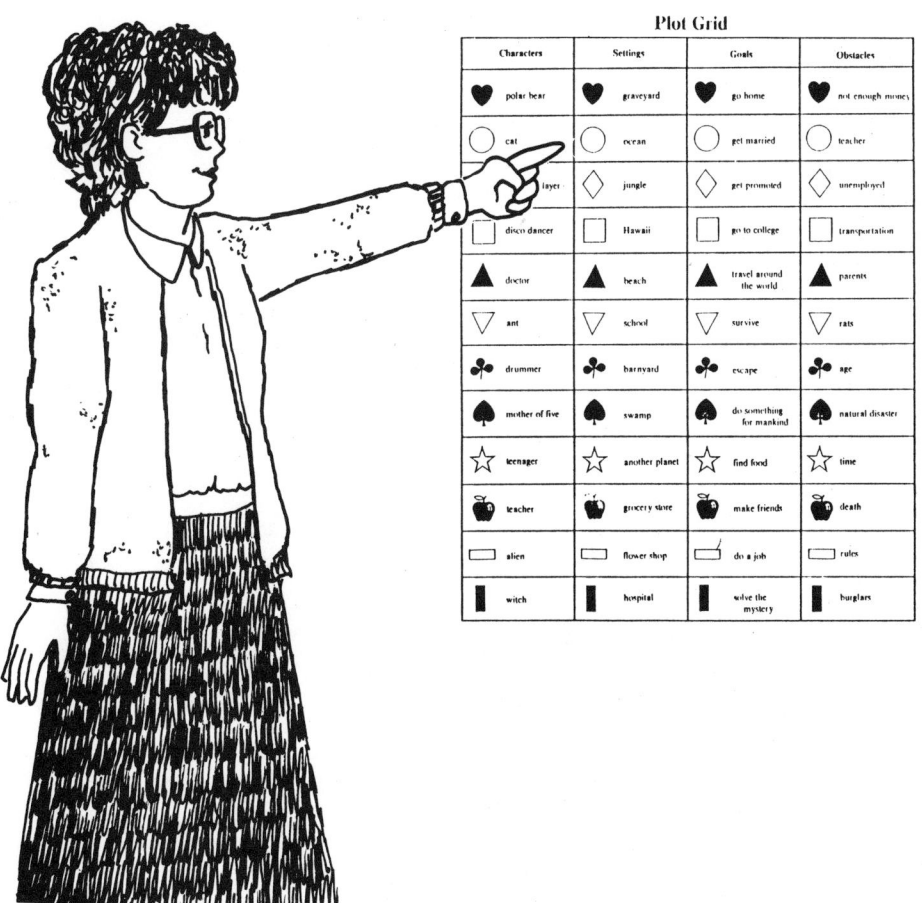

# Plot Grid

Directions: For a student to find his story's four main ingredients, follow the simple steps below.
1. Students make 48 cards from page 104. These may simply be cut from ditto paper or made stronger by backing them with tagboard and/or laminating.
2. Cards are shuffled facedown. (The symbols are the faces.)
3. Four cards are picked or laid down one at a time and placed down in order.

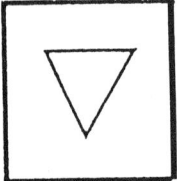   

4. The order matches the left-to-right order of the columns in the plot grid.
   The first card is the character.
   The second card is the setting.
   The third card is the goal.
   The fourth card is the obstacle.
5. Student matches the symbol in each column and writes a mini plot including the four ingredients he comes up with.

ant      swamp      go home      natural disaster

"After a terrible mud slide, Geraldo the ant, ended up atop an alligator in a swamp. To his dismay, he had no idea how he was going to get home, let alone off the alligator."

6. Students share their plot beginnings with one another.
7. At this time, the teacher may ask students to develop a more structured mini plot.
8. Students develop their mini plots into stories adding description, action and dialogue.
9. Any time the student wants a plot idea, he can shuffle his cards and select his plot ingredients. There are hundreds of possible combinations.

# Plot Grid

| Characters | Settings | Goals | Obstacles |
|---|---|---|---|
| ♥ polar bear | ♥ graveyard | ♥ go home | ♥ not enough money |
| ○ cat | ○ ocean | ○ get married | ○ teacher |
| ◇ football player | ◇ jungle | ◇ get promoted | ◇ unemployed |
| ☐ disco dancer | ☐ Hawaii | ☐ go to college | ☐ transportation |
| ▲ doctor | ▲ beach | ▲ travel around the world | ▲ parents |
| ▽ ant | ▽ school | ▽ survive | ▽ rats |
| ♣ drummer | ♣ barnyard | ♣ escape | ♣ age |
| ♠ mother of five | ♠ swamp | ♠ do something for mankind | ♠ natural disaster |
| ★ teenager | ★ another planet | ★ find food | ★ time |
| 🍎 teacher | 🍎 grocery store | 🍎 make friends | 🍎 death |
| ▭ alien | ▭ flower shop | ▭ do a job | ▭ rules |
| ▮ witch | ▮ hospital | ▮ solve the mystery | ▮ burglars |

# Plot Cards

Directions: Make into cards to go with plot grid. Each student should have four identical pages so he can make 48 cards.

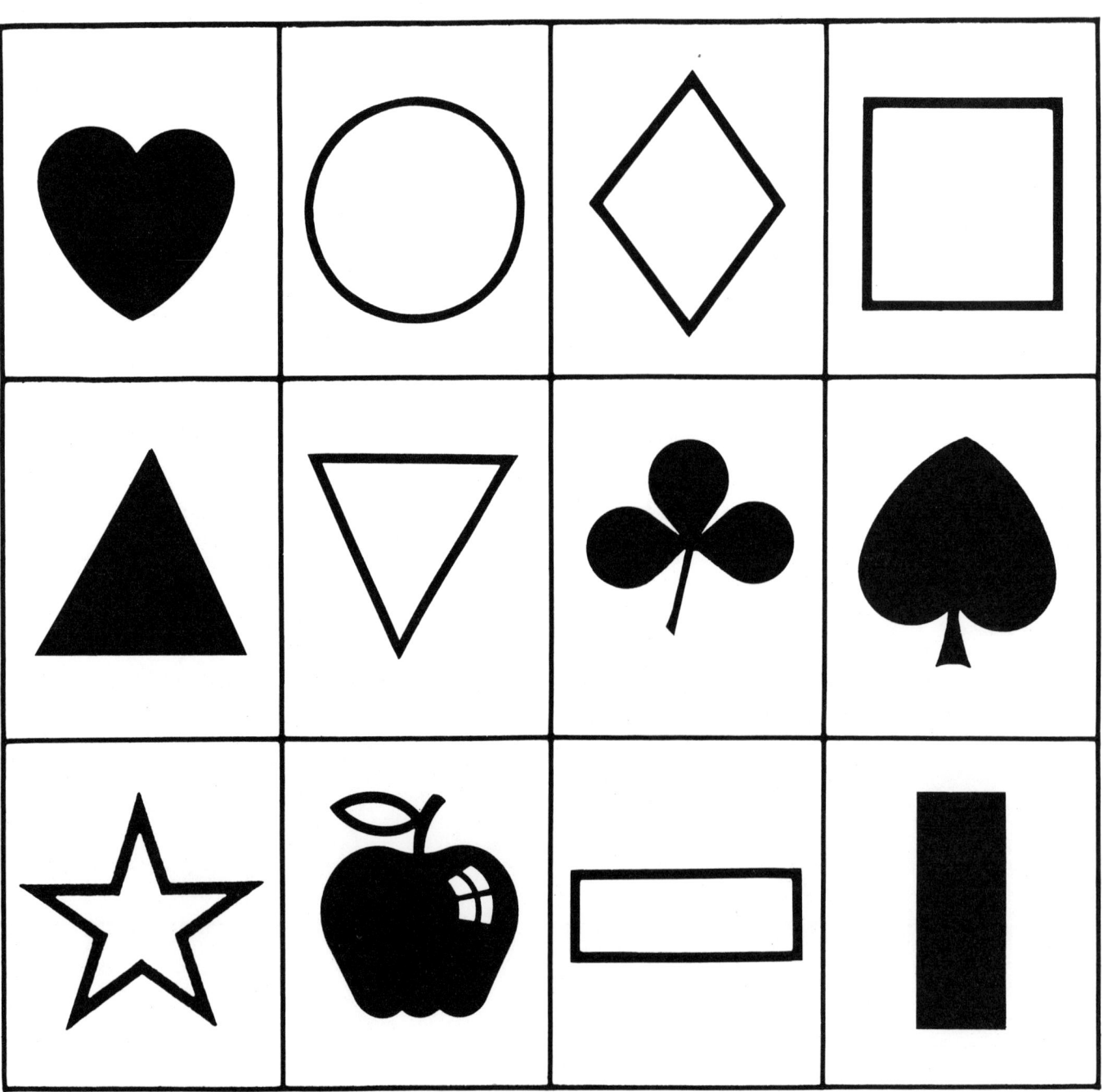

# Mini Plots

Activity: Given a choice of mini plots, each student will develop one into a story.

Materials: writing materials (writing paper, pencils)
mini plots on pages 106-109
author's development of a plot on pages 110-112

Objectives:
1. Students will leave out unnecessary detail that does not have anything to do with the plot.
2. Since other students may opt for the same plot, students will begin analyzing their own writing based on comparison with others.
3. Students will become aware of the structure of a plot.
4. Students will not have to worry about getting over the hump of designing a plot before they write.
5. Students will spend more emphasis on creating scenes in their writing.
6. Students will learn about criteria of developing plots into stories.

Directions: After the teacher explains to students they will be writing on one of the already structured mini plots designed for them, he/she goes over the criteria of developing the plot into a story.

1. Develop scenes about what is happening. Reader should know exactly what is going on.
2. Take the reader step-by-step through your plot.
3. Don't add information that has nothing to do with your plot.
4. Include description.
5. Include characterization.
6. Keep the reader in mind (RIM).

Teacher may use author's story on pages 110-112 in several ways:
1. As a warm-up example where students find examples of the criteria
2. After students have written "My Most Miserable Ten-Year-Old Day," include it as one to read to the class for analysis and discussion.

After students have written stories, the teacher may opt to read ones that meet the criteria. A good habit to get into at the conclusion of stories read in class is to ask students what the plot was or what the story was about in a few sentences or less.

# Mini Plots

Directions: Rewrite one of the mini plots below by creating the total event for the readers, so they feel like they are there. Include description of the scene and of the people. Include action and dialogue.

1. The old man and his devoted dog were told that some days you just shouldn't challenge that ocean. But he never listened. He breathed, lived and ate fish. One day there was a big battle between the sea and him, because a huge, terrible storm came up while he was at sea. Man and dog did not come back together that day.
2. It was the worst day in my ten-year-old life, one which I never want to repeat. From taking a cold shower—to eating a terrible breakfast—to missing my morning bus—to losing my assignment—to being unjustly accused of something I didn't do—to losing my best friend.
3. Amy wanted a cat so badly, but Mom always could think of excuses why she couldn't have one. One day, a starving kitten followed her home. From the moment she fed it, it wanted to adopt Amy. Mom kept saying "no." Cat and girl began winning Mom over as little girls and homeless cats can do.
4. Winifred and I went to our umpteenth dance. I don't know why; I guess we just like to watch everyone else have a good time. It proved to be the turning point in my romantic life, because there I met and danced with George.

# Mini Plots

Directions: Rewrite one of the mini plots below by creating the total event for the readers, so they feel like they are there. Include description of the scene and of the people. Include action and dialogue.

5. Jeremy decided he did not have any real friends. Everyone considered him the bully of the school. He decided one day he wanted friends, and the only way he was going to get them was to start being nice to everyone. However, it was a difficult day for him, because no one seemed to think the bully Jeremy was really trying to be nice . . . I mean not Jeremy!

6. My next door neighbors are Vietnamese, and I love to hear their heroic story of coming to America. First they went through the war, then a refugee camp. They finally escaped. Their biggest obstacle was crossing the sea in a small boat. When they finally arrived in America, they worked hard to get ahead.

7. Buster, a big Tom cat, was used to life in the alleys. He knew where the best scraps of food could be found and where to take cover from wind and snow. He was a survivor. He had fought for and protected his territory for years. This included protecting all the cats that had grown up as kittens in the area. One day Buster's life changed, because a kind old lady started feeding him and befriending him. She wanted to adopt him. In the long run he decided he couldn't leave his cat family that depended on him.

# Mini Plots

Directions: Rewrite one of the mini plots below by creating the total event for the readers, so they feel like they are there. Include description of the scene and of the people. Include action and dialogue.

8. Jennifer, a very shy sixth grader, for some time was noticing a very shy boy, Stephen, in her class. However, she was just too shy to begin any conversation with him though she had tried. Then when Valentine's Day rolled around, she bought him a very special card. However, just before school started, she decided she just couldn't go through with it, so she threw it in the wastebasket. Later, someone found it, and put it in the class valentine box. Stephen was delighted to receive the card. Because of it, he got enough courage to talk to Jennifer after school.

9. My family of five dragged me, an almost adult seventeen-year-old, on vacation and then to that children's world of wonder called Disney World. I was prepared for a most miserable time because of all I'd be missing back home. I pouted on the plane and pretty much ignored my surroundings the first day. Somehow, though, my vacation turned into the time of my life. I saw new worlds and met new faces. One face I'll never forget is Christie's. She helped me explore Disney World with a new attitude, and I even found more fun than snow skiing, which my friends back home were doing. I also realized my family could still be fun at seventeen.

# Mini Plots

Directions: Rewrite one of the mini plots below by creating the total event for the readers, so they feel like they are there. Include description of the scene and of the people. Include action and dialogue.

10. Everyone liked Joe, because he seemed to have everything going for him in Mrs. Weller's classroom—that is until the new boy arrived. The new boy seemed smarter than Joe and he had that sportsman's look. Through the course of the day, Joe struggles with his feelings about the class' over-enthusiasm with this new kid.

    Then during the afternoon recess, the new boy plays baseball with them and proves the better player than Joe. Joe is not nice to him, though the boy tries to be nice to Joe.

    Finally the new boy's niceness wins out when he nominates Joe for class president. Then Joe realizes he's not trying to steal the show, so he nominates the new boy for vice president. You can tell that they will soon be friends.

11. He had been a poor man all his life. He complained constantly if he only could win the lottery, life would be different. He'd get out from his miserable life as a poor man. Well, one day his luck turned around and he won the lottery. However, he found out that money doesn't alway bring happiness. It only brought on new problems for him. People, hoping for a taste of his fortune, wouldn't stop bothering him. His children became very spoiled. He couldn't decide what to do with all of his money, and everyone from attorneys (he didn't understand) to his relatives, had different suggestions. It got so bad, he just wanted to be poor again.

# My Most Miserable Ten-Year-Old Day*

*Mini plot #2 developed

# My Most Miserable Ten-Year-Old Day

B-E-E-P, B-E-E-P! "Uh-h-h." I didn't want to get up. B-E-E-P, B-E-E-P! 7:05. Oh please, only five more minutes of sleep. B-E-E-P, B-E-E-P! 7:10. I thought I heard Brad in the shower, so it wouldn't do me any good to get up then anyway. B-E-E-P, B-E-E-P! 7:15. "Elizabeth, get your body out of that bed this minute or you're going to be late for school. Elizabeth, did you hear me?"

"OK, OK," but Brad better be out of that shower. Through the bathroom door, I yelled at Brad to leave the shower on and to get out. (I didn't want to waste any minutes.) He bombarded out of the bathroom clad in a towel and said, "No problem, Sis." I just had time enough to give him my older-sister smirk before I dove into the shower. All of a sudden I was never so awake in all my ten-year-old life. Frigid cold bursts of water were biting my body all over. Why that good-for-nothing little brother! I shoved a slippery soap under my armpits and rinsed. Shaking from frostbite, I emerged from that eye-opener and grabbed for the towel. No towel! So I dried off with my pajamas and thus began the worst day of my life!

At that moment I should have gotten back into bed with pneumonia symptoms. But being the trouper I am, I dressed and went down for some warm breakfast. Cold oatmeal and hard, unbuttered toast greeted me. Todd had just gotten sick all over his high chair tray. I gnawed on my toast as my mother kept repeating, "Hurry up or you're going to miss your bus, and as you can see, I don't have time to take you to school. I tried to get up from the table, but she yelled, "Finish your breakfast, young lady." So I gnawed some more. After the toast was stuffed in my pockets and gagging cereal shoved down my throat, I left this miserable scene.

In record-breaking time, with schoolbag and lunch sack, I was out the door running towards the bus stop. As I approached my stop, my motor halted. No one was there, and I knew I wasn't early. I tried to convince my mom I honestly would stay in bed all day, but with motherly insistence and much disgust, she drove me to school. Todd drooled on me all the way to school as I worried about what Miss Wimbletondy would say.

The class was going over their English assignment on adverbs as I entered. "Good morning, Miss Tillman. Did you need a little extra shut-eye last night?"

"No, ma'am."

"Well, just give me your note and sit down." Note? My mom didn't write one.

"My mom didn't have time and the baby . . . ."

"I see, well take out your English assignment and join the class." I didn't dare look at anyone, so I stared in space as I made my way to my seat. You probably can guess the next part. With all the confusion of the morning, my English assignment was still on my dresser. "So, Miss Tillman, please give the answer to number seven."

"I don't know, Miss Wimble."

"Well, Elizabeth, your day isn't starting off very well, is it?" (An understatement.)

Staying in for recesses to do an assignment I already did isn't what I call a fun day. But then again, as I look back I wish I could have stayed in for three. Finally let out of prison, by the afternoon recess, I anxiously joined Susan and Rachel in a huddle by the swings. Susan and Rachel, are, or at least were, my best friends, so I wanted to know what I had missed.

"Well, we know Robby likes Rachel," said Susan, "because he's been staring at her in class."

"Well, well, what do you think about him, Rachel? I mean he's really pretty cool," I said.

Rachel took a deep breath and lowered her head, "OK. Now don't tell anyone you two, but being my best friends, I know I can tell you. I hope he does like me. I mean, he is cool."

Ding-a-ling, and we went in giggling, my first and last giggle of the day. I joined some girls in the bathroom and went into class. Mrs. Wimble was late, so we began whispering. From the back row I heard, "Rachel loves Robby. Rachel loves Robby." Naturally I wondered how anyone knew.

Before I had time to put any more thought into it, Rachel came storming up to me. In front of everyone she yelled, "Why you traitor! I'll never tell you anything again. You're no friend of mine."

"Rachel, I . . . ." I'm not sure what my next words would have been because in walked Miss Wimble. All I knew was that I was the most miserable ten-year-old in the world. What more could any ten-year-old take? I just lost my best friend . . . and for something I didn't do. I looked back at Susan for sympathy. She stuck her tongue out at me and made an awful face.

Tears started drip-dropping. Then came the sniffs and snorts. I'm sure I heard someone laughing. Miss Wimble asked to see me in the hall. Well, to make a long story short, I didn't ride the bus home either. Todd drooled all over me on the way home, too, but I cried all over him.

When we got home, Mom said she'd start a hot bath for me. I said, "No thank you." I just wanted to crawl back into bed with my big stuffed dog, Homer, and put the covers over my head. Mom said we'd have a talk later after my most miserable day ever was over.

# Unit V

# Developing Editing

# Introduction to Editing

This unit helps the student put together all the parts of a well-constructed story and through the editing process, refine the story to a more sophisticated level.

The author will guide the teacher and student through the development of one of her own stories using the strategies taught in this book. Examples of an eight-step writing process are included starting with a mini plot, sequential steps of the story and characterization examples. The fourth step included is the first writing draft utilizing the first three steps. The editing steps V, VI and VII have been combined for the reader's convenience. Editing in the form of symbols has been illustrated right on the original draft in this chapter. Because the author feels there is enough emphasis on spelling, grammar and punctuation, that kind of editing is not included in this book. It would be done also in the fifth through seventh steps.

The book concludes with the revised story, "Another Old Man and the Sea." Teacher and students alike should see evidence of improvement of the final to the draft.

The author originally wanted to use a student's piece of writing, because it would have been more realistic. Going through numerous students' works, it was difficult to find one where application of most all criteria of good writing could be used. All students have very individual writing strengths and weaknesses. Choosing any one student's writing would not have applicability to all students' writings. Thus the author wrote one herself in which she felt she could demonstrate editing in most all areas of need for good writing.

She also was able to be much more critical of her own writing for example purposes. Realistically, teachers should only edit what the teacher feels the child can handle and start out small by emphasizing the main area's need of improvement. For instance, if the student is not keeping the reader in mind (story is often unclear), emphasis should first be given to clearly structuring the story before more elaborate description.

# Steps to Writing Story

Step I:    Write mini plot.

Step II:   Write some action and dialogue for main characters.

Step III:  Write sequential steps from beginning to end to help plot evolve. Do not include steps that are not part of your plot.

Step IV:   Write story.

Step V:    Edit yourself. Read "Criteria of Good Writing" on pages 124 and 125 and improve where needed.

Step VI:   Read to class. Ask class suggestions on how to make story even better. After comments, take notes to refer to.

Step VII:  Teacher reads and edits.

Step VIII: Rewrite final story.

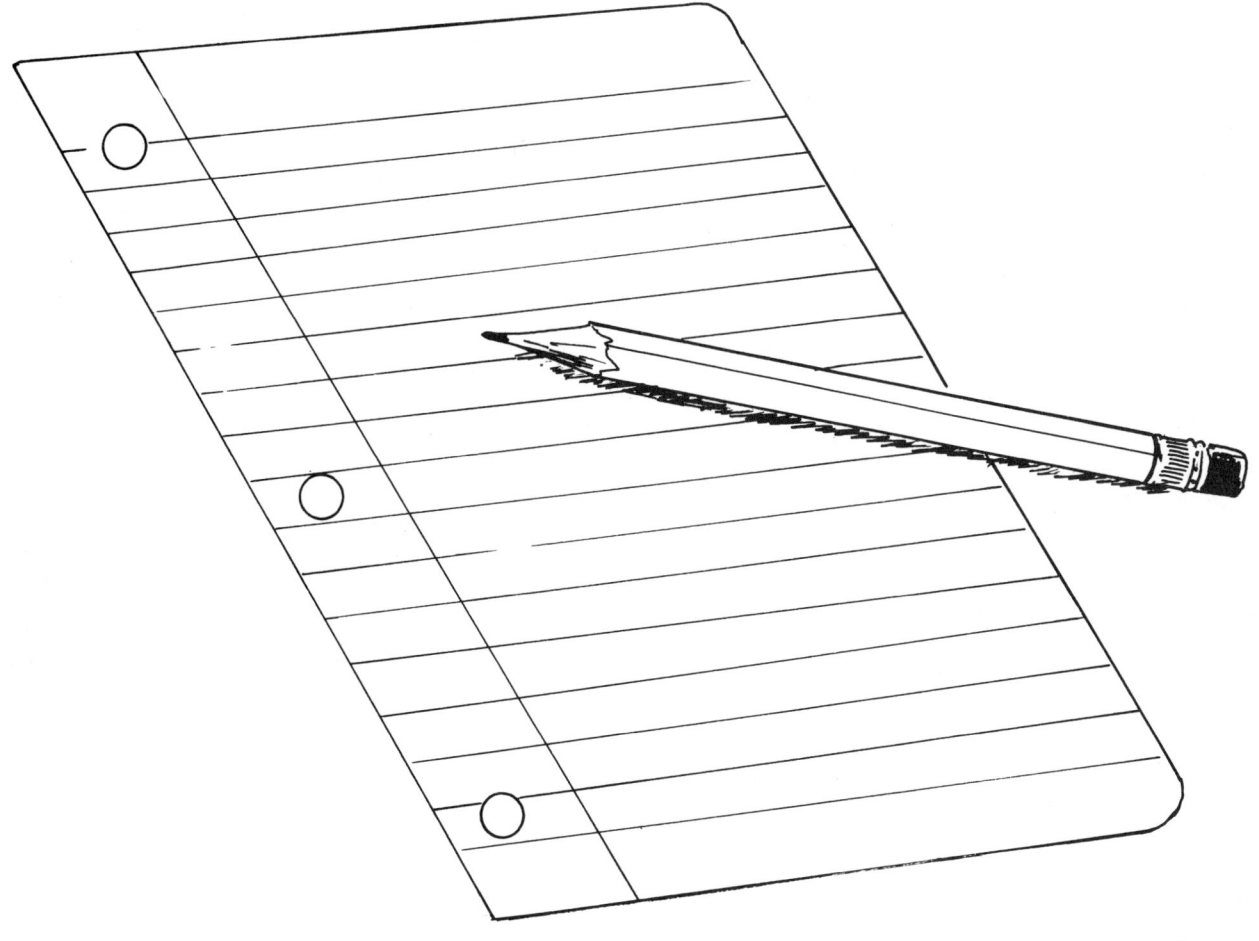

# Mini Plot for "Another Old Man and the Sea"

Step I: Writer summarizes his idea for a story from beginning to end in a paragraph.

A weathered old man and his dog are part of the routine of a small fishing town on the ocean. They go out to sea in the morning and come back at dusk. This is why Martha's Diner can claim "Fresh Catch of the Day." The old man just wants to mind his own business and be with his dog and the sea, but some teenagers hassle him and he can't ignore them. He and his dog get caught in a terrible storm, and the sea nearly beats them. The teenagers end up rescuing them. You can see at the end that the old man and the teenagers look differently at one another.

# Sequence of Events for "Another Old Man and the Sea"

Step II: Writer lists sequentially the main events in his story that support the plot.

1. Charlie and his dog go on their routine morning walk through town to his boat.
2. They stop at Martha's Diner which buys Charlie's fish.
3. People along the way warn him about the weather.
4. Teenagers hassle him.
5. In the water, the teenagers bother Charlie again, this time with their motorboat.
6. Charlie finally goes beyond where they want to go, because the storm begins to roll in.
7. He begins to fish.
8. Storm rolls in.
9. Charlie and Misfit battle the storm; it doesn't look good for them.
10. Charlie risks his own life to save his dog's.
11. The teenagers arrive just in time to save Misfit. They risk their own lives to dive after Charlie.
12. The next day things are pretty much back to normal, but Charlie and the boys seem to have a new understanding.

# Characterization

Step III: Writer brainstorms description, action and dialogue for main characters.

## Charlie

What is he like?  He is old and hardened maybe by a tough life; all he's got is his dog. His wife died a long time ago. He loves to fish. He has too much pride. He keeps pretty much to himself and the sea, except he is extremely loyal to his dog. He's grumpy and doesn't like to be bothered by most people. He doesn't think much of teenagers. He's nontrusting.

Action ideas:
- He ignores the children who talk to him.
- He fishes every day from sunrise to sunset.
- He ignores warnings about a storm coming up.
- He gets in a ruckus with some teenagers.
- He carries on conversations with his dog.
- He puts his dog's life before his in the storm.

Dialogue ideas:
- "Misfit, just igore those kids, and keep walking to the boat like I've told you before."
- "We been pals now for a long time" (to dog)
- "You boys, get out of my way."
- "Hang on, old boy. Just hang on." (during storm)
- "You boys should find something better to do than bother an old man."
- "Get out of here, and leave us alone!"

## Teenage Boys

What are they like?  You get the impression they are kind of bad but really they aren't. Maybe they're a little spoiled and get a charge out of teasing Charlie, but it's mainly because it riles him so. They are a little punkish and wild. One of them saves Charlie's life and helps him out at the end.

Action ideas:
- They tease Charlie.
- They try to get his dog from him.
- They throw his hat around.
- They make a lot of noise on their jet skis.
- They make big waves with their high-powered boat.

Dialogue ideas:
- "Here, Misfit. Come here, boy. Come away from the old man."
- "You just don't treat us with any respect."
- "Hey, here comes Old Man Charlie and his faithful pooch."
- "And that's all the thanks we get for saving his life."
- "Yea, I suppose, but I wonder what the old man's going to do now without his boat?"

# Misfit

What is he like?  He is very loyal to his master, though he's very much a typical dog. He loves kids, garbage and scraps. He's ten years old. He enjoys fishing with his master. He minds his master.

Action ideas:  Though he doesn't go to the kids, he gives signs like he would like to—wags his tail, cocks an ear. He sniffs garbage and walks around trees but never wanders far from his master.

Charlie

Misfit

teenagers

Rob

# Another Old Man and the Sea

# Step IV: Draft Before Editing

It is early morning and the sun is coming up. An old man and his dog are walking into a fishing village. The man is Charlie, and the dog is Misfit. They have been doing this every day for a long time, but no one knows where they come from. On their way to fish they stop at the restaurant where Charlie sells his fish. The owner warns Charlie about the weather and gives Charlie and his dog some food to take with them.

On the way to go fish, other people warn Charlie about the weather not looking very good, but he says he's not afraid. You see Charlie and Misfit have been going out to sea now for about ten years. Charlie's wife died and he boarded up his boat. When he found Misfit as a puppy left by his mother, he decided to open his boat up again.

Charlie seems grumpy when children try to talk to him and his dog.

"Hey, mister, what's your dog's name? Hey, mister?" says a little boy. Charlie ignores him and just keeps walking.

"Leave the old man alone," says the mother.

Finally nearing the dock, Charlie whispers, "Here comes trouble again. Misfit, just keep walking to the boat like I've told you before." Some teenagers begin bothering the old man.

"Here, Misfit. Come here, boy," three teenage boys yell while clapping their hands for Misfit to come. Misfit's tail wags and he keeps looking at the boys, but he stays by Charlie.

The boys start walking around Charlie. One boy with dark, curly hair and punkish says, "You spoiled that little boy's fun."

"That's my business, not yours. Now you boys get out of my way."

"Sure, old man, anything you say," says Rob, and he grabs Charlie's cap. The boys begin playing catch with it until it falls into the water.

Once safely on his old boat, Charlie and Misfit head out to sea. The sound of Charlie's motor is interrupted by a motorboat coming towards him. Charlie knows he can't outrun their motorboat, so he just motors on hoping they'll go away.

They go past him and begin cutting in front of him, making waves. He keeps motoring out to sea the best he can. This continues for quite some time. When the boys see lightning ahead, they turn for shore. "You'll be glad to know our fun's over for now, old man." They almost hit Charlie's boat as they turn back for shore. Charlie is calmed down by the time he fishes and sits next to his dog. Fishing proves good.

Charlie fishes for awhile. He reels in a little sunfish. Because it is small he lets Misfit have it. Misfit looks at Charlie as if to say, "Now where's another one?"

As Charlie throws his line in again, he notices the rising of the water. It slowly raises the front end of the boat and then the back. Misfit begins to whine slowly and then growls deeply within.

"I know, old boy, we're in for a big one this time. Hold on to your lunch. As Charlie reels in the line, the old boat takes a sharp dip backwards throwing Charlie backwards. He grabs for the wheel and pulls himself up. The boat begins rocking back and forth. Misfit whimpers and looks at Charlie for him to tell him what to do.

Terrible waves begin hitting the boat. Water starts pouring in. One huge wave rolls the boat on its side. Charlie searches for Misfit in the water. He finally finds Misfit and hauls him to a piece of boat sticking out of the water. "Hang on, old boy. Just hang on." The old man thinks he hears a motor in the distance. Maybe someone will rescue Misfit. No, it must be more thunder. Misfit slides toward the water. Charlie pushes him toward the middle. Charlie doesn't prop himself on what is left of the boat because he is afraid it will sink the rest of the way, and Misfit seems too weak to swim; he just doesn't want to chance it. However, Charlie is beginning to weaken, too. He recognizes the motor now, but his mind starts drifting from it. He begins sinking.

As the motorboat eases to the sinking boat, Rob yells, "There's Misfit, what's left of him." Misfit whimpers as the boys pull him to the safety of their boat. His whimpering becomes louder on the other boat. The boys begin toweling him off, but his whimpering only becomes louder. They finally realize he's worried about Charlie. "OK, Misfit, we'll see what we can do."

"Look, Rob, is that him?" They catch a glimpse of him just as a wave covers him. Rob dives in after the old man. Once he gets to him, surprisingly he doesn't fight him, other than repeating, "Get Misfit. Get Misfit."

"We got him, now come on, just relax and let me pull you in." Charlie is hauled in. Tom says, "You could have drown too, you know, Rob."

"Yea, I just didn't think." Everyone is silent on the way back.

Once back at shore, Charlie just walks off the boat. He grabs Misfit and says, "Thanks for saving my dog."

Tom looks at Rob and says, "And that's all the thanks we get. Doesn't he know you risked your life for him?"

"Yea, I suppose," says Rob. "But I wonder what the old man's going to do now without his boat?"

"Well, he's just lucky to be alive!"

The next day Charlie and his dog enter town as usual only this time, he is headed for the pier. He apologizes to Martha for not bringing her any fish yesterday.

"That's OK, Charlie, but are you all right?"

"Yea, me and my dog can still fish, only it's goin' to be off the old docks."

"Well, before you do that, you better go where you usually go. Rob and his dad are hauling in your old boat."

"Yea?"

"Yea, Charlie."

"Well, gotta go. Come on, Misfit. Looks like I was wrong about that kid."

Name _____

# Criteria of Good Writing
## (Student Resource Sheet)

Use descriptive language (adverbs and adjectives) if it helps picture something for the reader and/or makes it more interesting.

| Original | Revised |
|---|---|
| The very tall man and beautiful woman were looking at the flowers. | The towering gentleman and stunning lady were gazing at the kaleidoscopic posies. |
| The spider was glad the freezing rain stopped and the sun came out. | The glassy fibers of its web began to glisten as the sun peeked its head out. The web shivered as a droplet began to form and skimmy down a frozen web strand. |

Condense writing if you can say the same thing with fewer words.

| Original | Revised |
|---|---|
| The cat was very cold, because it was winter out. He wanted to be left inside. So he began crying at the door. He hoped someone would let him in soon. | The cold cat cried at the door, hoping somone would let him in soon. |

Use vivid language. The more exact picture the reader can see, the more he will be involved with the story.

| Original | Revised |
|---|---|
| I got up early. | My alarm went off at 7:01. |
| I heard my mom doing her exercises. | I heard my mom doing her exercises, "Thinner thighs when you Jazzersize." |

Vary words. Find a unique way of describing an overused pronoun or noun.

| Original | Revised |
|---|---|
| robot, he, a | metal-piece-of-junk, tin can |
| cat, he, it | flea varmint, furball |
| pollution, it | unnecessary garbage builder, environmental killer |

Name _____

# Criteria of Good Writing
## (Student Resource Sheet)

Keep reader in mind (RIM). Are you including enough details/description so reader knows what is happening?

### Original
Bowser just loved his new birthday present. Because of it, he stayed cleaner, and sometimes Mom let him in.

### Revised
Bowser just loves his new doghouse we bought him for his birthday. It's much better than his old one in that it is larger, has a floor and no holes in the roof. Now Bowser stays so much cleaner. Mom even lets him in our house sometimes, so Bowser really got two new houses.

Portray character traits through action and dialogue.

### Original
The witch was mean.

The little boy was scared.

### Revised
The crooked-looking old witch laughed her hyena laugh as she sprinkled school-hating dust on the children.

The little boy was trembling so hard he couldn't move.

Give examples if it is important to the story that the reader needs to be convinced strongly of something.

### Original
Arney loved rockets. One day he had a bad experience with a rocket.

### Revised
Arney loved rockets. Just from his room, you could tell his devotion to this hobby. Rocket models, ranging from miniatures to the giant one hanging from the ceiling, were all over. This boy wonder even had rocket sheets to sleep on. One day he had a bad experience with a rocket.

# Good Writing Criteria with Symbols

1. Use descriptive language (adverbs and adjectives) if it helps picture something for the reader.

    (*des.*) or ( ∧ ) insert descriptive words

2. Condense writing if you can say the same thing with fewer words.

    (*con.*) or ( < ) area to be condensed

3. Use vivid language. The more exact picture the reader can see, the more he will be involved with the story.

    ( _____ ) replace word underlined by using thesaurus

4. Vary words. Find a unique way of describing an overused pronoun or noun.

    ( ◯ ) around the overused words

5. Keep reader in mind (RIM). Are you incuding enough details/description so reader knows what is happening?

    (*RIM*)

6. Portray character traits through action and dialogue.

    (*char.*) (*act.*) (*dia.*)

7. Give examples if it is important to story that reader needs to be convinced strongly of something.

    (*ex.*)

8. Give sequential steps of things that happen if it is necessary for the reader's understanding.

    (*seq. step*) or (*ss.*)

9. Do not go off on tangents or ramble on about something that is not important to your plot.

    (*NIP*) or ( ✗ ) crossing out of area that needs eliminating

# Editing Reminders/Suggestions

1. It is recommended that this highly disciplined editing process be used only two or three times a year.

2. The steps in the process can be eliminated or rearranged as the teacher chooses.

3. When students are ready to verbally give editing comments, it is important the teacher prefaces it with, "What would you do to make the story even better?"

4. It lends a real comfort zone if the teacher shares his/her own writing and asks class to edit or at least make suggestions for improvement.

5. It is important for students to realize being a published author involves more than being a good creative writer; it involves perseverance and discipline which is demanded for editing and revision.

6. Student may comprehend #5 more by writing authors regarding the revision of their works. Having a guest writer (for example, from the press) may lend support.

7. The teacher should not edit harshly. Decide on main things student needs to work on and accentuate.

8. Just learning the criteria of good writing will help instill the practice.

9. It must be remembered it's a hard line to balance between having thoughts flow smoothly and being conscious of everything that should be included.

10. That's why editing is handled after the main writing. This means looking up words in a thesaurus, checking spelling, etc.

# Draft with Editing

*con.* — It is early morning and the sun is coming up. An old man and his/dog are walking into a fishing village. The man is Charlie, and the dog is (Misfit) *des.* They have been doing this every day for a long time, but no one knows where they come from. *(ex.)*

On their way to fish they stop at the restaurant where Charlie sells his fish. The

*dia.* — owner warns Charlie about the weather and gives Charlie and his dog some (food) *ex.* to take with them.

On the way to go fish, other people warn Charlie about the weather not looking *dia. & ex.* very good, but he says he's not afraid. You see Charlie and Misfit have been going

*dia.* — out to sea now for about ten years. Charlie's wife died and he boarded up his boat. When he found Misfit as a puppy left by his mother, he decided to open his boat up again.

Charlie seems grumpy when children try to talk to him and his (dog.) *char./ex.*

*good! More* — "Hey, mister, what's your dog's name? Hey, mister?" says a little boy. Charlie ignores him and just keeps walking.

"Leave the (old) man alone," says the mother.

Finally nearing the dock, Charlie whispers, "Here comes trouble again. Misfit, just keep walking to the boat like I've told you before." Some (teenagers) begin bothering the (old) man.

*little more des. — boys*

*More act. & dia.* — "Here, Misfit. Come here, boy," three (teenage) boys yell while clapping their hands for Misfit to come. Misfit's tail wags and he keeps looking at the boys, but he stays by Charlie.

The/boys start walking around Charlie. One boy with dark, curly hair and punkish says, "You spoiled that little boy's fun."

"That's my business, not yours. Now you boys get out of my way."

"Sure, old man, anything you say," says (Rob,) *RIM* and he grabs Charlie's cap. The boys begin playing catch with it until it falls into the/water. (RIM) *(act.)*

A (RIM): *There's no mention of Charlie being upset.*

(so.) Once safely on his old *new* boat, Charlie and Misfit head out to sea. The (sound) of Charlie's (motor) is interrupted by a (motorboat) coming towards him. Charlie knows *more des.* he can't outrun their (motorboat,) so he just (motors) on hoping they'll go away.

They go past him and begin cutting in front of him, making waves. He keeps (motoring) out to sea the best he can. This continues for quite some time. When the boys } RIM see ^(so.) lightning ahead, they turn for shore. "You'll be glad to know our fun's over for now, old man." They almost hit Charlie's boat as they turn back for shore. (des.)

A (RIM) Charlie is calmed down by the time he fishes and sits next to his dog. Fishing proves good.

*Write more fishing scene* { Charlie fishes for awhile. He reels in a little sunfish. Because it is small he lets Misfit have it. (RIM) Misfit looks at Charlie as if to say, "Now where's another one?"

As Charlie throws his line in again, he notices the rising of the water. It slowly raises the front end of the boat and then the ^back. Misfit begins to whine slowly and then growls deeply within.

"I know, old boy, we're in for a big one this time. Hold on to your lunch. As Charlie reels in the line, the (old) boat takes a sharp dip (backwards) throwing Charlie (backwards.) He grabs for the wheel and pulls himself up. The boat begins rocking back and forth. Misfit whimpers and looks at <u>Charlie</u> for him to tell him what to do.

<u>Terrible</u> waves begin <u>hitting</u> the boat. Water starts pouring in.(so) One <u>huge</u> wave rolls the boat on its side. Charlie ^searches for Misfit in the water. He finally finds Misfit and hauls him to a piece of boat sticking out of the water. "Hang on, (old) boy. Just hang on." The (old) man thinks he hears a motor in the distance. Maybe someone will rescue Misfit. (so) ar No, it must be more thunder. Misfit slides toward the water. Charlie pushes him (RIM) toward the middle. (RIM) Charlie doesn't prop himself on what is left of the boat, because he is afraid it will sink the rest of the way, and Misfit seems too weak to swim; he just doesn't want to chance it. However, Charlie is beginning to weaken, too. He recognizes the motor now, but his mind starts drifting from it. He begins sinking. (ex.)

As the motorboat eases to the sinking boat, Rob yells, "There's Misfit, what's left of him." Misfit (whimpers) as the boys pull him to the safety of their boat. His (whimpering) becomes louder on the other boat. The boys begin towling him off, *[you or not realistic]* but his whimpering only becomes louder. They finally realize he's worried about Charlie. "OK, Misfit, we'll see what we can do."

"Look, Rob, is that him?" They catch a glimpse of (him) just as a wave covers (him.) Rob dives in after the (old) man. Once he gets to (him,) surprisingly he doesn't fight (him,) other than repeating, "Get Misfit. Get Misfit."

"We got (him.) Now come on, just relax and let me pull you in." Charlie is hauled in. (RIM) (Tom) says, "You could have drown too, you know, Rob."

"Yea, I just didn't think." Everyone is silent on the way back. *(RIM) what's happening to nearly dead Misfit?* Once back at shore, Charlie just walks off the boat. He grabs Misfit and says, "Thanks for saving my dog."

Tom looks at Rob and says, "And that's all the thanks we get. Doesn't he know you risked your life for him?"

"Yea, I suppose," says Rob. "But I wonder what the (old man's) going to do now without his boat?"

"Well, he's just lucky to be alive!"

*(ex.)*

The next day Charlie and his dog enter town as usual only this time, he is headed for the pier. He apologizes to Martha for not bringing her any fish yesterday. *(dia.)*

"That's OK, Charlie, but are you all right?"

"Yea, me and my dog can still fish, only it's goin' to be off the old docks."

"Well, before you do that, you better go where you usually go. Rob and his dad are hauling in your (old) boat."

"Yea?"

"Yea, Charlie." *(Can you let reader interpret this on his own from something Charlie says?)*

"Well, gotta go. Come on, Misfit. Looks like I was wrong about that kid."

*Note: The amount of editing on these pages is for example purposes only. Students' papers should not be edited to this extent.

# Examples of Types of Individual Comments

Good plot; stuck to it fairly well

Needs more description: old man, boys, storm scene, Charlie and Misfit fishing

Go over words to see if they are as vivid as you can make them.

Overused words: old, whine, whimper

Can reader find this out through dialogue?

Examples of more sophisticated types of individual comments:
(depending where student is with his writing and what he can handle)

Reader needs to see what is going on all the time (for example, walking down to fish, Charlie and Misfit fishing).

Can you bring in more about the discord between the boys and Charlie? Why don't they get along, and if they don't, why don't the boys leave him alone?

# Another Old Man and the Sea
## (Revised Story After Editing)
### by Melissa J. Donovan

# Another Old Man and the Sea
## (Revised Story)

In front of the sun coming up is a silhouette of a man and his dog. As it breaks into daylight, the figures become an old weathered man and his shaggy sidekick. Charlie and Misfit enter the fishing village as usual every morning. No one knows exactly where they come from, an abandoned cottage, a tent or a mansion, but they've been coming for years. They make their way down to the wharf to fish. First they stop at Martha's Diner that advertises "Fresh Catch of the Day" in its window. A squarish woman greets Charlie at the door. "Come on back; I'll make you a sandwich or two, and I've got some scraps left for Misfit. How'd you like that, old boy? Doesn't the sky look strange to ya, Charlie?"

"Yes, but I've seen worse in my day."

Not taking very long, because Charlie is anxious to start his day, he emerges from Martha's Diner with two paper bags in hand, one for him and one for Misfit. There's much activity early in the fishing village, but Charlie and his dog pretty much walk through it. Misfit is distracted often by trees and garbage but always keeps his eyes on his master, who keeps shuffling along, confident his companion is close behind.

"How's the fishing been, Charlie?" yells Mr. Crimshaw from his market across the street.

"Keeps me and my dog alive."

"Well, if you get any really big ones, let me know."

"Yep."

"Charlie, do you think you should get a weather report before going out today? Doesn't look right to me."

"Nope."

"OK. Safe traveling."

"Weather report? How long you and me been going out now, Misfit? Ten years now, and there wasn't a day we couldn't handle. Yea, you're part of the sea too— you born on old *Clemsy* and all. I member boarding her up for good when Clara died. Your mama musta known it was a safe place to have you, though I don't know where she went. Anyway, when I found you, I thought it was time to open the boat again."

"Hey, mister, what's your dog's name? Hey, mister?"

Charlie just keeps scuffling along.

"Leave the old man alone, Joey."

"Mama, Mama," yells a younger child, "Is that Santa?"

"Santa, Santa," a little pigtailed girl runs up to Charlie. Charlie speeds up his walking a little. The little girl sadly goes back to her mother.

"That is no Santa Claus, Annie, because Santa would never be such a grump. Mother grabs Annie's hand to scurry off, and the little girl turns around and says, "Bye, doggie."

Finally approaching the dock, Charlie whispers, "Here comes trouble again. Misfit, just keep walking to the boat like I've told you before."

"Here, Misfit. Here, Misfit. Come here, boy, three tanned teenage boys yell while clapping their hands for Misfit to come. Misfit's tail vibrates and he keeps looking at the boys, but he stays at the heels of his master.

"OK, OK, boy, we know O'Charlie's got the chains on you and spoils all your fun. Isn't that right, Charlie? Hey, Charlie, isn't that right?" demands the long-haired boy.

"I don't think he heard you, Rob." The athletic looking punks stride over to Charlie. The boys begin their jive type walking around Charlie.

"Come on, Charlie. Where's your Christmas spirit?" says Rob, his earring catching the sun's rays. Strong muscles protrude through his shirt. "You spoiled that little girl's fun."

"That's my business, not yours. Now get out of my way. You boys should find something better to do than bother an old man and his dog. Don't any of you hold down regular jobs?"

"Come on, it's summer vacation, man. Anyway, our life's the sea, just like yours."

"Yea, being the marina owner's son and seein' how fast you can go on the water in that fancy boat of yours."

"It's time to go," says the cropped-hair boy named Tom. "He's right; we have better things to do."

"I don't think so. He just doesn't treat us with respect like we deserve." With that, Rob grabs Charlie's cap and sends it through the air to one of the other boys.

"Give me my cap, you good for nothin' generation."

"Sure, old man, anything you say." The cap swishes in the air over Charlie's head and into the murky water. By the time he bends over to get it, it disappears below. Someone hands him a boat hook, and he pokes it into the water. Once he retrieves the soggy hat, he plops it dripping on his head. The boys disappear.

Once safely on his old wooden trawler, Charlie and Misfit head out to sea. The gentle purr of Charlie's motor is interrupted with r-r-rn-ow, r-r-rn-ow, r-r-rn-ow. He sees a motorboat zigzagging towards him. As it gets closer, it glides in the air, bounces on the water and glides again. Charlie knows he can't outrun their speedboat, so he motors on hoping they'll go away. They surpass him and begin cutting in front of him, making waves his boat isn't used to. He keeps plowing on out towards the sea, up over the waves, the best he can. This continues for quite some time. When lightning streaks the sky up ahead, the boys turn for shore. As they get near Charlie's boat, they appear to be coming right into it. Within inches of hitting it, they veer left, spraying water in the crack between the two boats.

"You'll be glad to know, old man, our fun's over for the day. The sky looks mean up ahead, but the stupid old man you are, you'll probably stay out here. But why don't you let O'Benj come with us. He doesn't want to get caught in this, do you?" Misfit cocks an ear.

"Just get out of here and leave us alone," Charlie shakes his fist.

Charlie calms down as he slows the motor. He is ready to sit next to his faithful companion and fish. Fishing proves good.

"Hey, Misfit, another one," says Charlie as the fishing rod pulls his arms over the boat. Charlie slowly reels the little sunfish in as it flip-flops against the nonstirring waters.

"Not too big, Misfit, but it should be a mighty tasty appetizer for ya." As the sea-weathered, hunched-over man wrestles with the slimy piece of last minute life, his shaggy companion's saliva drools from his mouth. The brown, cracked hand throws Misfit the fish. It is gone after an immediate catch, two bites and one big swallow. Misfit looks at Charlie as if to say, "Now where's the main course?"

"It's coming. It's coming," says Charlie. As he throws another worm-adorned line into the water, he notices the swelling of the water. It slowly raises the front end of the boat and then gracefully dips it forward with the sea. Misfit begins to whine slowly and then growls deeply within.

"I know old boy, we're in for a big one this time. Hold on to your lunch." He hastens reeling in the line. With the last turn of the reel, the ancient boat takes a sharp dip backwards, throwing Charlie against the stern. He grabs the wheel and pulls himself up. Big masses of clouds move in overhead. The boat begins rocking back and forth. Misfit whimpers and looks at his master for him to tell him what to do.

"We've got to take her on. We have no choice. Nope—just you and me against the sea. Come here and I'll fasten you to the boat, because she's coming in pretty strong now."

Charlie reaches out toward Misfit as the boat lurches upward. Then it smashes downward, and Misfit rolls to the back of the boat. Vicious eight-foot waves begin pounding the boat. Water begins pouring in and Misfit bobs like a wet mop from side to side. One massive wave and the boat rolls on its side. Charlie frantically splashes in the water looking for Misfit. His hand grabs a mass of fur and hauls it to a protruding piece of boat sticking out of the water. "Hang on, old boy. Just

hang on." The old man thinks he hears a motor in the distance. Maybe someone will rescue Misfit. No, it must be more thunder. The storm finally begins to calm. Misfit lies limp on the boat sticking out of the water. When he slides toward the water, Charlie pushes him towards the middle. Charlie doesn't prop himself on what is left of the boat, because he is afraid it will sink the rest of the way, and Misfit is too weak to swim in the water. He just doesn't want to chance it. But Charlie is weakening. He pushes Misfit to the middle and slides himself under the water. Then he bobs up again. The storm is mostly over, but the waves are still swells. Each one begins to take Charlie further away from Misfit.

He recognizes the motor now, but his mind starts drifting from it. He grabs for the wood, but it isn't there. He begins sinking. As the speedboat eases to the half-visible boat, Rob yells, "There's Misfit; what's left of him. Curse that stupid old man." Misfit whimpers as the boys pull him to the safety of their boat. His whimpering becomes louder on the other boat.

"OK, OK, we'll see if the old guy is still around."

"Look, Rob, is that him?" Charlie gasps for breath but is still partially afloat. All of a sudden, a big wave covers him again. Rob dives in. Once he gets to him, surprisingly Charlie doesn't struggle other than repeating, "Get Misfit. Get Misfit!"

"We got him. Now come on, just relax and let me pull you in. Now hang on to this life ring." Charlie is hauled in. As the two boys help Rob aboard, Tom says, "You could have drown too, you know, Rob."

"Yea, I just didn't think." Everyone is silent on the way back. The sun begins to peek out, and Misfit shakes himself letting everyone know he's all right.

Once back at shore, Charlie staggers off the boat. He grabs Misfit and murmurs, "Thanks for saving my dog."

Tom looks at Rob and says, "And that's all the thanks we get. Doesn't he know you risked your life for him?"

"Yea, I suppose," shivers Rob. "Now, I wonder what the old gizzards going to do? His boat's in the middle of the lake, probably pretty torn up by now."

"Well, he's lucky to be alive if you ask me!"

"But his life is the sea."

The next day man and beast enter town at sunrise. Charlie has an old fishing pole over his shoulder and is carrying a bucket. As he passes Martha cleaning tables outside, he says, "Sorry 'bout yesterday, Martha; the fish just weren't biting."

"I heard, Charlie. You OK?"

"Yea, I got my mutt, and the sea's still at our feet. We'll just have to do our fishing off the old docks."

"Well, before you do that, you better go down where you usually go. There's a lot of commotion going on. Rob Spinster and his dad have been hauling in an old trawler that got pretty wrecked at sea yesterday."

"Yea?"

"Yea, Charlie."

"Well, gotta go. Come on, Misfit, we got a big day's fishin' ahead. Besides gettin' our usual catch for Martha, bet the Spinsters would like a fish dinner tonight."

# Answer Key

**Thesaurus Crossword Warm-Up** page 12

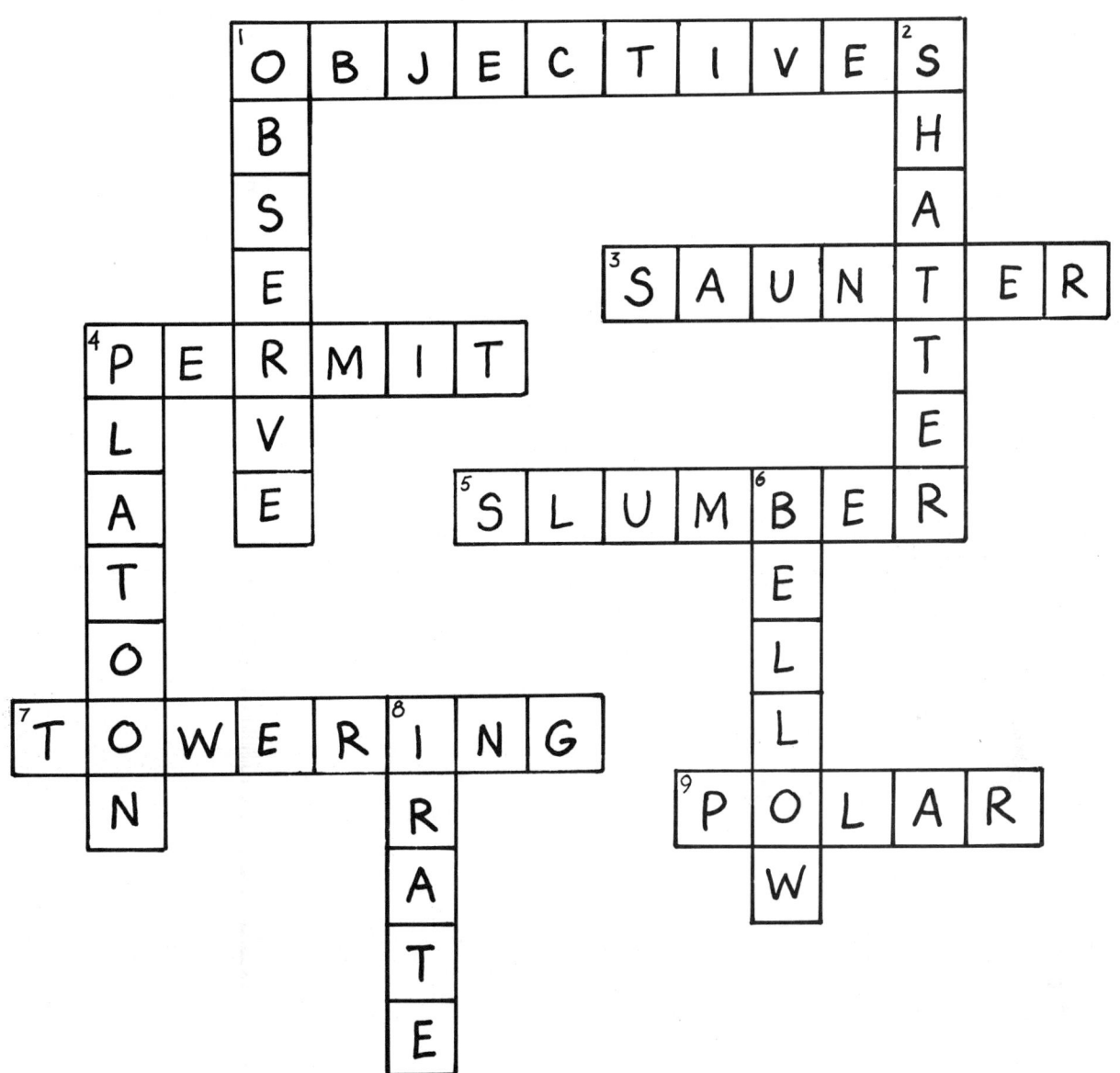

**Time for Sentences** page 22

Sample answers:
1. The plotting old codger trailed the bedraggled shaggy and starving pooch with his crooked cane.
2. The robust and snuggly bundled tots withstood extraordinary knee-high weather conditions and wisking frozen vapors to create an impressive snowman.
3. A popular annual trip for our family is to the Holland Tulip Festival, where we see a multitude of glorious tulips in diverse technicolor.
4. The unsightly ebony spider promenaded without risk around his web, making stock of his apprehended, dangling victims.
5. I deserve the energizing position; I'm dedicated, genuine and highly principled; tidy and careful with detail; and just a simple, caring all-around fellow.

**Characterization Work Sheet** page 74

Sample answers:

Dialogue of a Kind Person:
1. "Even though you can't hit the ball, Jeremy, we like you."
2. "Mom, I'll help you with the dishes."
3. "Hello, George, I just called to see how you were feeling."
4. "I'm sorry. I didn't mean it."
5. "Here, let me help you with the heavy package."
6. "I know how you feel. That's happened to me before."
7. "Hey, Pam! Come and join us. You probably can help us find a faster way of doing this."
8. "Please."
9. "Thank you."
10. "You may not be good in sports, but I sure wish I had your brain, any day."

Action of a Kind Person:
1. picks up something someone drops
2. waits for a friend
3. brings someone sick their schoolwork
4. doesn't have to be first
5. includes someone who is alone in a group
6. compliments others
7. cheers someone who is down
8. helps someone who doesn't understand something
9. sticks up for the underdog
10. makes sure no one is left out
11. lets someone with one item go ahead in line at the grocery store
12. apologizes for inconsiderations or misunderstandings
13. doesn't put others down
14. makes people feel good about themselves

# CONTENTS

Introduction . . . . . . . . . . . . . . . . . . . . . . . . . . . 4

**Tall Tale**
Pecos Bill Finds a Ranch but Loses a Wife . . . . . . . 7
The Story Behind This Tall Tale . . . . . . . . . . . . . . 17

**Native American Tale**
The Turkey Girl . . . . . . . . . . . . . . . . . . . . . . . . 19
The Story Behind This Native American Tale. . . . 31

**Ethnic Tale**
The Flower of Life . . . . . . . . . . . . . . . . . . . . . . 33
The Story Behind This Ethnic Tale . . . . . . . . . . . 45

**Regional Tale**
Running with the Mustangs . . . . . . . . . . . . . . . . 47
The Story Behind This Regional Tale . . . . . . . . . 54

Read, Research, and Write . . . . . . . . . . . . . . . . 55

Extend Your Reading . . . . . . . . . . . . . . . . . . . 56

INTRODUCTION

# What Are Folktales?

Folktales are stories that are passed down from one generation to the next. They are tales told by ordinary people around campfires, kitchen tables, or anywhere else people gather to swap stories. Folktales are a part of every culture because telling and listening to familiar stories helps people belong to a group.

A folktale begins as a spoken tale. It can change each time it is told. Storytellers are free to add details to make the story funnier or more exciting. In this way, folktales can be shaped by the person telling the story.

# Types of Folktales

There are different types of folktales. There are stories about people, animals, and the land. Some stories are about monsters or magic. There are tall tales about characters who perform unbelievable tasks. Or trickster tales with clever heroes who outsmart others.